THE ALMIGHTY FORMULAE

Abraham 'Wole Haastrup

THE ALMIGHTY FORMULAE

Abraham 'Wole Haastrup

Published in Australia by
Sunrise Foundation International (SFI).

The Almighty Formulae

Copyright @ 2015 by Abraham 'Wole Haastrup

ISBN 978–0–992-3823-3-9

All rights reserved. No part of this book may be produced, stored in a retrieval system, or transmitted in any form or by any means — electronic, mechanical, photocopy, recording, scanning, or any other — except for brief quotations in printed reviews, without the permission of the publisher.

Unless otherwise indicated, Scripture quotations are from The New King James Version of the Holy Bible, copyright 1982 – Thomas Nelson, Inc. used by permission.

Published in Melbourne, Australia by
Sunrise Foundation International (SFI)
c/o 32, Blueberry Street, Greenvale Gardens,
Victoria 3059, Australia.

Other Books by the same author:

- God Still Speaks Today

- High Praise

- Obedience- The Secret of Miracles

- In Remembrance of Me

- Your Last Hope

- The Secret of Divine Favour

- Ebenezer (God Can Do It Again)

- The Christian Worker

- Nations At Rage

Table of Contents

Introduction

1. The Shout of Triumph
2. God Will Make You Laugh
3. You Can Dream Again!
4. The Almighty Formulae
5. The Wind of Change
6. The Untouchables
7. The Man Called Simon
8. Help On The Way
9. Divine Visitation
10. Divine Encounter
11. Christian Commitment
12. Victory At the Gates!

OPEN HEAVENS - Matters Arising

Afterwords

Acknowledgements

Introduction

The word 'Almighty', refers to someone or something that possesses absolute power, strength, & might. Such object or being can accomplish anything & everything it wants, at anytime & anywhere it wants. This means the one called or described as the 'Almighty' is not & cannot be limited by time, space, resources, & age.

Without any doubt, the only one in heaven & earth who qualifies to be so described is GOD. Our God is the ALMIGHTY. How do we know that He is?

First, He described Himself so. Gen 17:1 & Deut 32:39 both declare:

"And when Abram was ninety years old and nine, the LORD appeared to Abram, and said unto him, I am the Almighty God; walk before me, and be thou perfect...

See now that I, even I, am he, and there is no god with me: I kill, and I make alive; I wound, and I heal: neither is there any that can deliver out of my hand."

Second, His works prove that He is the Almighty. For

example, Creation itself. In Gen 1: 1-3, we read:

"In the beginning God created the heaven and the earth. 2 And the earth was without form, and void; and darkness was upon the face of the deep. And the Spirit of God moved upon the face of the waters. 3 And God said, Let there be light: and there was light."Romans 1:18-20 also says: "18 For the wrath of God is revealed from heaven against all ungodliness and unrighteousness of men, who hold the truth in unrighteousness; 19 Because that which may be known of God is manifest in them; for God hath shewed it unto them. 20 For the invisible things of him from the creation of the world are clearly seen, being understood by the things that are made, even his eternal power and Godhead; so that they are without excuse" (see Psalm 24:1-4).

Third, His very actions show clearly that He is the Almighty. For example, Psalm 115:3; Psalm 8:1-2 tell us:

"But our God is in the heavens: he hath done whatsoever he hath pleased... O LORD our Lord, how excellent is thy name in all the earth! who hast set thy glory above the heavens. 2 Out of the mouth of babes and sucklings hast thou ordained strength because of thine enemies, that thou mightest still the enemy and the avenger."

Fourth, His wisdom is great & unsearchable. Rom 11:33-36 says:

"33 O the depth of the riches both of the wisdom and knowledge of God! how unsearchable are his judgments, and his ways past finding out! 34 For who hath known the mind of the Lord? or who hath been his counsellor? 35 Or who hath first given to him, and it shall be recompensed unto him again? 36 For of him, and through him, and to him, are all things: to whom be glory for ever. Amen."

The word 'formulae', has many connotations. It is said to be 'a symbolic expression of the structure of a compoud'. 'Formular' has also been defined as 'a prescription, solution, or plan of action'. It can therefore mean a key or a code, oran equation. For example, in the subject of chemistry, water is represented by "H2O". On the other hand, "CO2" is used to represent carbon dioxide. In the same manner, the equation "A2+B2=C2" is very familiarly known as 'the Pythagoras Theory'. A Formular can also be a strategy.

Many organizations or companies will tell or reveal only common or obvious things they do. They will rarely let out their real strategies, or the key elements of their products, or what makes them 'thick' and unique! The Coca Cola company is one of such global outfits that does this.

Also, a Formular can mean the reason or explanation behind an action. That is, the cause that leads to an effect. For instance, behind every curse, there must have been a violation of a stated law of God. The same is true of blessings. For there to be an easy & unhindered flow of a blessing, there must be or have been some obedience. The Bible declares in Gen 22:11-18 & Mal 3:8-12:

" 11 And the angel of the LORD called unto him out of heaven, and said, Abraham, Abraham: and he said, Here am I. 12 And he said, Lay not thine hand upon the lad, neither do thou any thing unto him: for now I know that thou fearest God, seeing thou hast not withheld thy son, thine only son from me. 13 And Abraham lifted up his eyes, and looked, and behold behind him a ram caught in a thicket by his horns: and Abraham went and took the ram, and offered him up for a burnt offering in the stead of his son. 14 And Abraham called the name of that place Jehovah-jireh: as it is said to this day, In the mount of the LORD it shall be seen. 15 And the angel of the LORD called unto Abraham out of heaven the second time, 16 And said, By myself have I sworn, saith the LORD, for because thou hast done this thing, and hast not withheld thy son, thine only son: 17 That in blessing I will bless thee, and in multiplying I will multiply thy seed as the stars of the heaven, and as the sand which is upon the sea shore; and thy seed shall possess the gate of his enemies; 18 And in thy seed shall all the nations of the earth be blessed; because thou hast obeyed my voice... 8 Will a man rob God? Yet ye have robbed me. But ye say, Wherein have we robbed thee? In tithes and offerings. 9 Ye are cursed with a

curse: for ye have robbed me, even this whole nation. 10 Bring ye all the tithes into the storehouse, that there may be meat in mine house, and prove me now herewith, saith the LORD of hosts, if I will not open you the windows of heaven, and pour you out a blessing, that there shall not be room enough to receive it. 11 And I will rebuke the devourer for your sakes, and he shall not destroy the fruits of your ground; neither shall your vine cast her fruit before the time in the field, saith the LORD of hosts. 12 And all nations shall call you blessed: for ye shall be a delightsome land, saith the LORD of hosts."

In Matthew 6:3-4, we also learn:

"3 But when thou doest alms, let not thy left hand know what thy right hand doeth: 4 That thine alms may be in secret: and thy Father which seeth in secret himself shall reward thee openly."

The same goes for failure, losses, death, etc. When any of these occur, there must have been some negligence, carelessness or other causes.

When we talk about the Almighty Formulae therefore, we are talking about the strategy of God, His master key, or His equation, & His unsearchable wisdom that is far beyond human or scientific calculations. God operates by principles. The principles formed the basis for what we can call His Formulae. All formulae that ever worked are based on standard principles. In the earthly realm, some principles do not work because the necessary & sufficient conditions are not fulfilled. Things are different with God. His formulae works everywhere, in all places, & all the time! For example, getting or becoming blessed requires that we truly know God. In Daniel 32:11c, the Bible says: *"And such as do wickedly against the covenant shall he corrupt by flatteries: but the people that do know their God shall be strong, and do exploits"*.

The NIV renders it this way: *"With flattery he will corrupt those who have violated the covenant, but the people who know their God will firmly resist him (i.e, the devil)."*

There are some critical things to know about God. These include His person, His character, His principles, His purpose, & His plans. It is also critical to know His timing, His placement and/or location (Psalm 103:7).

The words 'strong' & 'exploits' in the above Text, can respectively be interpreted to mean 'confident' & 'prosper' or to be 'heroic' or 'achieve an extra-ordinary deed'. For example, knowing God's Name is necessary for our safety, promotion, progress and advancements (see Proverbs 18:10; Psalm 91:1).

This book - The Almighty Formulae - is a collection of faith-inspiring messages. The book will surely renew your confidence in the Almighty God. The book catalogues the diverse ways which God uses to intervene in the affairs of those who belong to Him. As you go through it, may the Almighty God release unto you the secret & strategy for success, breakthrough & total freedom in Jesus Name, Amen.

CHAPTER 1

THE SHOUT OF TRIUMPH
(John 19:30)

A **SHOUT** has been described as a sudden and loud outcry. In general, people shout to attract attention and/or help. The truth however, is that different people have different reasons why they shout.

For example, some people shout because they are afraid or they are frightened. A few years ago, a woman came in the middle of a rainy night banging our entrance door shouting "Pastor, Pastor, they have come again!" We opened and she jumped in sweating, with her three children. I asked her: "who are the 'they' and 'where are they?" Eventually, we followed her to her nearby Apartment. She pointed to the back of her window. We looked and saw nothing and no one. We however prayed with her and her children, and God gave them peace from every fear – real and imaginary!

Some people also shout because they are in pain. Just a visit to the Emergency or Labour Wards of a Hospital will make this real to you. Some other people shout because they are excited. Just go near a football field or Stadium and hear the Fans when their team has just netted in the ball. On the other hand, some people shout when they receive some good news, say, a letter of promotion, a wife's safe delivery, or the result of an examination. Lastly, some people shout as a result of regret, when they come face to face with their error or foolishness.

Beside all these, there is a special shout that is called 'The Shout of Triumph'. That is what God wants you and me to keep on shouting everyday of our lives. May this be our portion in Jesus Name. The Bible says in Psalm 47:1-2: *"Oh clap your hands, all you peoples! Shout to God with the voice of triumph! For the LORD Most High is awesome; He is a Great King over all the earth."*

All across the Bible, we can see and hear this type of shout: In Luke 2:8-14, when our Lord Jesus was born, there was a shout of triumph because Light entered a world so filled and full of darkness, to dispel it. Jesus Himself, said in John 8:12:

"Then spake Jesus again unto them, saying, I am the light of the world: he that followeth me shall not walk in darkness, but shall have the light of life."

When He was here physically, everywhere Jesus went, He performed miracles, and when miracles happened there were shouts of triumph. We can see this vividly in John

5:1-9; John 9:1-7, and John 11:41-44. In Mark 6:1-56 alone, Jesus performed four special miracles that caused great shouts of triumph. I don't know in what area of your life you are believing or trusting God for divine intervention. Even as you read this book, may the Lord step in and cause you to shout the shout of triumph in Jesus Name.

In Matt 21:7-11, Jesus rode to Jerusalem & the crowd shouted:*"Hosanna to the Son of David, Blessed is He who comes in the Name of the Lord, hosanna in the highest"*. It was a shout of triumph!

When Jesus hung on the Cross and shouted 'IT IS FINISHED', it was a shout of triumph. This was because finally, He had accomplished the main reason for which He came into the world. I John 3:5-8 says:

"5 And ye know that he was manifested to take away our sins; and in him is no sin.

6 Whosoever abideth in him sinneth not: whosoever sinneth hath not seen him, neither known him.

7 Little children, let no man deceive you: he that doeth righteousness is righteous, even as he is righteous.

8 He that committeth sin is of the devil; for the devil sinneth from the beginning. For this purpose the Son of God was manifested, that he might destroy the works of the devil."

Three times, the devil attempted to trick Jesus out of the primary purpose of His earthly journey (see Matt 4:1-11; Matt 16:21-23; Luke 22:40-44). As Satan failed over Jesus, may he continue to fail over your life and my life in Jesus Name.

Eventually, Jesus went to the Cross on our behalf. However, His death on the Cross, His burial & being in the grave for three days were NOT His end. On the third day HE arose from the dead! Mark 16:1-8 says:

"1 And when the sabbath was past, Mary Magdalene, and Mary the mother of James, and Salome, had bought sweet spices, that they might come and anoint him. 2 And very early in the morning the first day of the week, they came unto the sepulchre at the rising of the sun. 3 And they said among themselves, Who shall roll us away the stone from the door of the sepulchre. 4 Andwhen they looked, they saw that the stone was rolled away: for it was very great. 5 And entering into the sepulchre, they saw a young man sitting on the right side, clothed in a long white garment; and they were affrighted. 6 And he saith unto them, Be not affrighted: Ye seek Jesus of Nazareth, which was crucified: he is risen; he is not here: behold the place where they laid him. 7 But go your way, tell his disciples and Peter that he goeth before you into Galilee: there shall ye see him, as he said unto you. 8 And they went out quickly, and fled from the sepulchre; for they trembled and were amazed: neither

said they any thing to any man; for they were afraid."

In I Corinthians 15:12-20, Apostle Paul made it clear that: *"12 Now if Christ be preached that he rose from the dead, how say some among you that there is no resurrection of the dead? 13 But if there be no resurrection of the dead, then is Christ not risen: 14 And if Christ be not risen, then is our preaching vain, and your faith is also vain. 15 Yea, and we are found false witnesses of God; because we have testified of God that he raised up Christ: whom he raised not up, if so be that the dead rise not. 16 For if the dead rise not, then is not Christ raised: 17 And if Christ be not raised, your faith is vain; ye are yet in your sins. 18 Then they also which are fallen asleep in Christ are perished. 19 If in this life only we have hope in Christ, we are of all men most miserable. 20 But now is Christ risen from the dead, and become the firstfruits of them that slept."* BUT thank God Jesus rose and He is alive today, and forever more (see also Rev 1:18).

Whenever a new soul is won for the Lord, there is a shout of triumph in Heaven:"Likewise, I say unto you, there is joy in the presence of the angels of God over one sinner that repenteth." (Luke 15:10).

Also, whenever a Christian resists Satan and overcomes sin, there is a shout of triumph in Heaven – by the Clouds of Witnesses. Heb 12:1-3 asserts:

"1 Wherefore seeing we also are compassed about with so great a cloud of witnesses, let us lay aside every weight, and the sin which doth so easily beset us, and let us run with patience the race that is set before us, 2 Looking unto Jesus the author and finisher of our faith; who for the joy that was set before him endured the cross, despising the shame, and is set down at the right hand of the throne of God. 3 For consider him that endured such contradiction of sinners against himself, lest ye be wearied and faint in your minds."

There still remains 2 special shouts of Triumph:

At the 2nd coming of the Lord Jesus – when He returns soon. I Thess 4:16-18; Rev 1:7 reveal thus:

"16 For the Lord himself shall descend from heaven with a shout, with the voice of the archangel, and with the trump of God: and the dead in Christ shall rise first: 17 Then we which are alive and remain shall be caught up together with them in the clouds, to meet the Lord in the air: and so shall we ever be with the Lord. 18 Wherefore comfort one another with these words... 7 Behold, he cometh with clouds; and every eye shall see him, and they also which pierced him: and all kindreds of the earth shall wail because of him. Even so, Amen." As a Christian, are you looking forward to His soon coming? (see John 14: 1-3; I John 2:28-29; I John 3:1-3).

The Final Shout of Triumph will be at the Coronation of our Lord Jesus, when He will rewarded for all He did formankind. It is often said that 'He who laughs last, laughs best'. On the cross, the shout of triumph by our Saviour was with pains and agony. Thank God, this last and final shout of triumph will be glorious and with great joy:

"9 After this I beheld, and, lo, a great multitude, which no man could number, of all nations, and kindreds, and people, and tongues, stood before the throne, and before the Lamb, clothed with white robes, and palms in their hands; 10 And cried with a loud voice, saying, Salvation to our God which sitteth upon the throne, and unto the Lamb. 11 And all the angels stood round about the throne, and about the elders and the four beasts, and fell before the throne on their faces, and worshipped God, 12 Saying, Amen: Blessing, and glory, and wisdom, and thanksgiving, and honour, and power, and might, be unto our God for ever and ever. Amen." (Rev 7:9-12).

There is another side to all we have been discussing thus far. It is a shout of regret! Unfortunately, some people have been shouting it, and some will still shout it at the end of the age.

In Genesis 3:23-24, when God drove Adam and Eve out of the Garden of Eden, they must have shouted a shout of regret! It must have dawned on them that disobedience especially to God and His word have grave consequences. However, it was already too late for them! May we all make our ways right with God before it becomes too late for us in Jesus Name.

In Judges 16:20-21, when the Philistines plucked out the two eyes of Samson, he would have shouted the shout of regret, realizing that he could not eat at the Lord's Table and the table of Satan all at the same time:

"20 But I say, that the things which the Gentiles sacrifice, they sacrifice to devils, and not to God: and I would not that ye should have fellowship with devils. 21 Ye cannot drink the cup of the Lord, and the cup of devils: ye cannot be partakers of the Lord's table, and of the table of devils. 22 Do we provoke the Lord to jealousy? are we stronger than he?" (I Cor 10:20-22).

Also, he must have realized that he cannot carry God's anointing, be messing up with sin, and at the same time expect to get away with it! II Tim 2:19 & Rom 6:1-2 declare:

"Nevertheless the foundation of God standeth sure, having this seal, The Lord knoweth them that are his. And, Let every one that nameth the name of Christ depart from iniquity...1 What shall we say then? Shall we continue in sin, that grace may abound? 2 God forbid. How shall we, that are dead to sin, live any longer therein?"

Gehazi too, in II Kings 5: 25-27, must have shouted the shout of regret when he suddenly became a leper and his destiny got altered forever as a result of covetousness.

The same goes for Judas. In Matt 27:3-6, he must have shouted the shout of regret when he discovered that the 30 pieces of silver he got for selling/betraying his Leader was useless.

In recent times, great men and women in public and religious circles have shouted the shout of regret when suddenly, the Law of Harvest caught up with them and their secret sins of several years came to the open (see Matt 6:4). The question for you, Dear reader, is: What shout do you want to shout at the end of your life - the shout of triumph or the shout of regret? Matt 7:21-23 says:

"21 Not every one that saith unto me, Lord, Lord, shall enter into the kingdom of heaven; but he that doeth the will of my Father which is in heaven. 22 Many will say to me in that day, Lord, Lord, have we not prophesied in thy name? and in thy name have cast out devils? and in thy name done many wonderful works? 23 And then will I profess unto them, I never knew you: depart from me, ye that work iniquity." (See also Matt 25:19-30; Luke 16:19-31; Rev 20:10-15).

The Bible adds in I Tim 5:24-25:

The Almighty Formulae

"24 Some men's sins are open beforehand, going before to judgment; and some men they follow after. 25 Likewise also the good works of some are manifest beforehand; and they that are otherwise cannot be hid."

It is not too late to make amends. Begin today, and now. May the Lord have mercy on us all at His coming in Jesus Name!

CHAPTER 2

GOD WILL MAKE YOU LAUGH
(Gen 18:9-15)

In Gen 18:14, a Question was asked by an Angel: *"Is there anything too hard for God?"*

Something provoked that question - it was the laughter of Sarah - Abraham's wife. She had been barren for several years. Now, she & her & husband, Abraham had become very old & advanced in age (Vs 11). Then, she overheard the Angel saying to her husband: "This time, next year, Sarah your wife shall have a son"! Then she laughed within herself.

There are many types of laughter:

There is the laughter of excitement. It may be provoked by a joke, or an experience. For e.g., as a lover of soccer, when your Team scores a goal or wins a match.

There is a cynical laughter. This can be due to unbelief (Gen 17:17; 18:12; Gen 37:5-11, 18-19; II Kings 7:1-2).

There is also the laughter of naked man - someone insane.

When he sees other people well dressed, he would laugh out of wonder - imagining that something must be wrong with the one who was not naked like him! There is the laughter you laugh at a fool - the one who says there is no God, or people who think they are smarter than God. Such people eat their cake & yet want to have it back! They don't obey God, yet they want God to bless them.

They think they can hide some things from the all-seeing God - the One who called Himself "the Alpha & Omega (Matt 6:4; Rev 1:8).

Finally, there is the laughter of Divine Intervention. You laugh it when God surprises you at a time or point when you have lost all hopes, or HE did something far beyond your expectations. The same Sarah later laughed this type of laughter in Gen 21:6 when she was carrying her Isaac in her hands. As you read this book, in a miraculous way, God will put in your hands your long-awaited miracle & you too will laugh the laughter of divine intervention in Jesus Name.

May be you look at your self & it became clear or obvious that you have passed the age prescribed for a particular grant or entitlement. This not withstanding, God will still surprise you! He will make a way for you in Jesus Name. The young man called Joseph may have laughed the laughter of divine intervention on many occasions in his life. For instance in Gen 41:43, when he rode on a horse &

was being taken round the whole of Egypt as the new Prime Minister & second-in-command to King Pharaoh. Brigadier- General & Mrs Potiphar would have been part of the people commanded to "bow the kneel" as Joseph passed. Also in Gen 50:18, when his brothers prostrated for the fifth time to him, Joseph would have laughed & probably sang " O Lord my God, when I awesome wonder..".

What of Hannah? She too must have laughed the laughter of divine intervention when she gave birth to Samuel. I believe the same is true of David (see Psalm 126:1-5). Our Daddy, the General Overseer of the RCCG paid a PastoralVisit to Australia in November 2013. A Sister sowed a gift to the life of God's Servant. According to her, the money she gave was meant for re-registration for a qualifying examination she had just written. She was ready to re- register for the exam because she was sure she wrote 'nonsense' in the exam! A few weeks after her gift to the Gen Overseer, the result came & she passed very well! By God's grace, I have had some challenges in life & ministry. Some time in 1989, I was completely overlooked & my name kept off a list of officers to be nominated for an oversees course. This was in spite of my being very qualified. Somehow, God intervened when all chances had gone. The boss who engineered the 'conspiracy' was suddenly transferred out of our Department! The new boss recalled & reviewed the list. I was included & the proposal sailed through. I pray for you as you read this, "Every force (human & spiritual) that has been positioned to rob you of your destiny shall be relocated in Jesus Name".

Not too long ago, I was posted to a particular part of my home-country where God has tremendously prospered His work through the Mission with which we are serving.

Ordinarily & on the surface all seemed well. When the time to resume was near, we made an advanced trip there to see the one from whom I was taking over. Then the day to officially resume came, & we began work. Less than two weeks a group of people entered my office led by a high ranking officer in the system. Without mincing word, their leader told me that they had come as representative of the larger body to "tell you that we don't want you here"! Now, if this had happened to me while I was in secular employment, I wouldn't have been bothered at all. But this in a Church - my own Church, the church that believed & preached holiness, & what we must do to make it to Heaven at last! Ithank them for coming & for whatever group or interests they represented. I however made it clear to them that I did not lobby to be posted to them! To cut short a long story, God stepped into the matter, & we ended up spending 5 solid years in the place. We were transferred out of the place with what one can describe as a triple promotion! I remember very well that when we returned from the Annual Convention of that Year (and many of my 'friends' had already heard the announcement about my promotions), we were given a heroic welcome! There is an adage that says "He who laughs last, laughs best"! Are you going through some tough situations? God will see you through & make you laugh.

As you are reading this book, it may be that you used to laugh so easily & so freely before. Then something happened & your laughter disappeared. Today, God will make you laugh again. He will restore your laughter in Jesus Name.

There are some basic truths about life: First, with men & for men, some things are very hard & difficult (II Kings 2:9-10). Second, some things are not only hard & difficult for men, they are in fact impossible with men (Matt 19:26). One may then ask the question: Why are some things hard or difficult & impossible with men? The answer is simple: MEN ARE HIGHLY LIMITED! Let me show you what I mean. A man wanted to help his friend who was in need. He asked him to come a few days later. Just a few days to the time he wanted to make the help available, he himself was sacked from office. Consequently, he could not help his friend!

Some years ago, I was very concerned for a Sister (a widow) in our Fellowship. I asked her to see me the following day in my office. That very night, on getting home, I developed an ailment. I became so sick that for thefollowing sixty-three (63) days I couldn't even step of my house not to talk of going to the office. Thank God with Him, NOTHING is too hard.

With God too, NOTHING is IMPOSSIBLE (Luke 1:37)! What limits men do not limit God. He cannot be sick, He cannot be sacked. He cannot lack resources. He does not sleep nor slumber. He does not travel, He cannot die. In addition, His phone line does not have voice-mail. His line has no network problem. He still hears & answers prayers. May He hear & answer you today in Jesus Name?

The only thing that can hinder Divine intervention is sin - particularly the sin disobedience, unbelief & doubt. Why don't you bow your head right away & ask God for mercy (Prov 28:13). You may also join in praying the following prayer points:

Father, thank You for this day of Your truth. Thank You for who You are - the Almighty - the One for whom nothing is too hard.

Father, please forgive me anything that can hinder You from stepping into my case. Forgive my disobedience, please have mercy on me.

Father, please visit me today & make me laugh. Father, please turn all my impossibilities to possibility.

CHAPTER 3

YOU CAN DREAM AGAIN!
(I Chronicles 4:9-10)

Did you once have a dream? - Perhaps a great goal or a high ambition - to be somebody in life, to be great or on top in your Career, your profession, or even in Ministry & God's Service? Have you been 'caught in the wind' & the dream has been lost? I pray that God will restore your dream in Jesus Name.

Perhaps like one of the seeds sown by the Sower in Mark 4, you have realized that you are among 'thorns' &'chokers' - the cares of this world & the deceitfulness of riches have derailed you. May be you have joined people who think that more & more money can give peace & fulfillment. Or you have joined yourselves to people who think money can buy anything & anyone including God! - people who have forgotten that the life of a man does not consist in the abundance of what he possesses (Matt 6:33; Luke 12:15).

May the Lord open your eyes and help you to re-order your priority aright in Jesus Amen.

Are you downcast, lukewarm or discouraged by the hypocrisy in the Church - among members, church or Christian Workers, & even leaders (both Ministers, Pastors,& denominational leaders)? Are you out of fellowship with God, and with men? Perhaps you have gone to a 'new' church to hide in the crowd even though you carry the anointing & vision in your life, may you dream a new dream. May that dream of greatness - to be somebody for God in your generation - be rekindled again in Jesus Name! YOU WILL DREAM AGAIN! You will be who God designed you to be (Ephes 1:10-11; Rom 8:28). In Jer 29:11, God told the backslidden Israelites:

"For I know the thoughts that I think toward you, says the LORD, thoughts of peace and not of evil, to give you a future and a hope".

May the good thoughts of God concerning you & you family become a reality in Jesus Name.

Let us begin by asking some important questions:
1.   What is a dream?
2.   What happened to the original dream?
3.   Where & how did it happen?
4.   Where am I Now?
5.   Can I dream again?

May the Lord speak to us all in Jesus Name (Amen)!

Someone said, 'A dream is what you see or experience when you fall asleep, especially at night'. Unfortunately when some people lie down at night, it is "good night Jesus"! - they see nothing, or when they wake up they don't remember what they dreamt about - whether good or bad.

That can be very dangerous.

Dreams are important. They have many sources as well as purposes. They can be pointers to what God or the Devil is out to do in a man's life or around him.

In Gen 28:10-18; Gen 37:5-11; Gen 40:1-22, God released some vital information that had to do with destinies, of individuals & Nations. In Matt 2: 12-23, through dreams, God gave warnings to the 3 Wisemen as well as Joseph concerning the Baby Jesus, who King Herod was desperately out to kill.

While I often warn people never to be enslaved by what they dream about at night, particularly if it is negative, I equally advise that we should not ignore our dreams. Praise God for His Word, it is far, far superior, & it overrides all dreams! We are to pray into reality positive dreams, while using the Word of God to counter all dreams & every negative dream.

It is also said that 'A Dream is what you see which has the effect of taking away sleep from your eyes"! That is, what you see with your inner eyes became a passion, - a pursuit, and/or a wake up call. In Acts 9:1-9, a man called Saul of Tarsus had an encounter with Jesus & he was never the same again. What he saw & Who he met brought him under a New Management. It was also a wake up call. It made him realize how close to hell he was (I Cor 15:8-10; 1 Tim

1:12-17). That singular encounter also gave him a new direction & pursuit in life:

"7 But what things were gain to me, those I counted loss for Christ. 8 Yea doubtless, and I count all things but loss for the excellency of the knowledge of Christ Jesus my Lord: for whom I have suffered the loss of all things, and do count them but dung, that I may win Christ, 9 And be found in him, not having mine own righteousness, which is of the law, but that which is through the faith of Christ, the righteousness which is of God by faith:10 That I may know him, and the power of his resurrection, and the fellowship of his sufferings, being made conformable unto his death; 11 If by any means I might attain unto the resurrection of the dead.12 Not as though I had already attained, either were already perfect: but I follow after, if that I may apprehend that for which also I am apprehended of Christ Jesus. 13 Brethren, I count not myself to have apprehended: but this one thing I do, forgetting those things which are behind, and reaching

forth unto those things which are before, 14 I press toward the mark for the prize of the high calling of God in Chris Jesus." (Phil 3:7-14).

A Dream has also been said to be "That which you think, see or desire - a vision or an aspiration, - a goal".

For many people, & also for you, the first or original dream may have become dimmed, hijacked, or completely forgotten altogether! This can be due to several factors.

For some, it was due to an evil association. I Cor 15:33 says:

"Be not deceived: evil communications corrupt good manners."

When a man becomes unequally yoked, he will lose his dreams.

In Psalm 11:3, we read *"If the foundations be destroyed, what can the righteous do?"* (See also II Cor 6:14-18; Psalm 1:1-3).

For some, it was complacency - the pride of 'I have arrived'. May be this is why you in particular had lost your dreams. Your 'good' have become the enemy of your 'best'. To some people, it was comfort - they became so comfortable that they lost direction & Fire. They refused to leave their 'comfort zone'. Hence, Apostle Paul told himself (as quoted earlier),:

"12 Not as though I had already attained, either were already perfect: but I follow after, if that I may apprehend that for which also I am apprehended ofChrist Jesus.13 Brethren, I count not myself to have apprehended: but this one thing I do, forgetting those things which are behind, and reaching forth unto those things which are before," (Phil 3:13-14).

Yet, for some people, it was the foolishness of comparing themselves with others! - vain competition. "Mr 'A' has bought a new Jeep, built a new & bigger house, I too must have my own". To such people, acquiring what others had, have become an end in itself (I Cor 10:12).

Some people also lost their dreams because they began to share God's glory, & that became their ruin. God simply withdrew or departed from them. Then failure & frustration set in. God said in Isa 42:8:

"8 I am the LORD: that is my name: and my glory will I not give to another, neither my praise to graven images." (see also Psalm 127:1; John 15:5).

There are some who lost their dreams because they out rightly went into some sins. Are you one of them?

Have you been trapped in some open or secret sins? May be you are even right now 'in the laps of a Delilah' - in adultry of fornication (Judges 16:18-21). The several pregnancies you have aborted or assisted your sin-partner to abort should grieve your heart!

- You may also be in some business or transactions that are totally unbiblical & unchristian. As you are reading this book, you may even have walked into a trap & be under some form of captivity. Perhaps the enemies are already mocking you - asking you to 'sing to them the Lord's song in a strange land' (Psalm 137:1-4). Is there any hope for you? The answer is YES! You can dream again! Can you?

YES, you can! Among other things, I believe the following steps will surely help you to return to, and recover your dream as well as your destiny:

First, you must come to your senses! When the young man the Bible described as the Prodigal Son requested for his own portion of the father's inheritance and left home, he probably had a big dream. However, he was 'caught in the wind'! He took many wrong steps & got into the company of too many wrong people. The Bible in I Corinthians 15:33 (Contemporary English Version) says:

"33 Don't fool yourselves. Bad friends will destroy you!" Thank God for His mercies. In Luke 15:14-17, the Bibles says *"14 And when he had spent all, there arose a mighty famine in that land; and he began to be in want. 15 And he went and joined himself to a citizen of that country; and he sent him into his fields to feed swine. 16 And he would*

fain have filled his belly with the husks that the swine did eat: and no man gave unto him. 17 And when he came to himself, he said, How many hired servants of my father's have bread enough and to spare, and I perish with hunger!"

In other words, he came to his senses - his understanding returned. He suddenly realized that he was in the wrong place, with the wrong people, and doing the wrong things. Let's hear him again in verse 17:

"How many of my father's hired servants have enough bread & to spare, & I perish with hunger".

Here, he began to dream again! He went down memory lane & saw how degenerated he had become both physically, materially, mentally &spiritually. He did not stop there, in Vs 18-19, he went on, *"I will arise & go to my father, & will say to him, "Father, I have sinned against heaven & before you, and I am no longer worthy to becalled your son. Make me like one of your hired servants".*

You too need to come to come to yourself. You need to come to your senses. You need to arise & return to God your Father. He is the only One who can help you dream again. He is the only One who can restore your destiny Ephes 1:11 says: *"In whom also we have obtained an inheritance, being predestinated according to the purpose of him who worketh all things after the counsel of his own will."*

Second, you must repent. You need a change of heart that will be manifested by a change in your actions (Isa 55:6-7 & Prov 28:13 both declare:

"6 Seek ye the LORD while he may be found, call ye upon him while he is near: 7 Let the wicked forsake his way, and the unrighteous man his thoughts: and let him return unto the LORD, and he will have mercy upon him; and to our God, for he will abundantly pardon

13 He that covereth his sins shall not prosper: but whoso confesseth and forsaketh them shall have mercy."

Third, you must come out of the evil you are in at present (II Cor 6:14-18).

It is a sign that you are ready & prepared to move on in a new & positive direction.

Fourth, you must ask God for mercy. You must ask Him to restore you, and restore your dream, as well as your destiny. He is a God of second chance. In I Chronicles

4:9-10, a man called Jabez prayed a very important prayer. Something led to it. He too once had a dream. Along the line, some things happened & he lost it. However, he realized something must have been wrong somewhere.

The Almighty Formulae

He took a wise decision to bring his case to God - the God of Israel, & that God stepped into his case. As you too returnto God, may He step into your case & give you a brand new start in Jesus Name.

Finally, you must make today your day to return to God (II Cor 6:2).

The first step in your restoration is an assurance of your relationship with God (John 1:11-14; John 3: 3-5).

You may want to be guided by the following prayer points:

- Father, forgive me for all the doors I have opened for the devil (I Peter 5: 7-9).

- Father, from now on, I make You my No 1 (see Matt 6:33).

- Father, every ground I have lost, please restore to me.

- Help me never again to lose focus.

- Father, give me a new dream

- Father, if I am wrongly located now, please relocate me & give me a new beginning.

- Father, every untouchable thing I have touched, I restitute my ways.

CHAPTER 4

THE ALMIGHTY FORMULAE
Isaiah 40:14-18

It will not be out of place to begin this chapter with some very important questions. For example, Who indeed is the Almighty God? Can He be known? Has He in any way revealed Himself?

The Agnostics said God can not be known because He has not made Himself available for study or to be known. This is a great deception, & they are totally wrong! The truth is, God can be known. In fact He has revealed Himself very clearly.

Rom 1:18-20 & Psalm 103:1-5 declare:

"18 For the wrath of God is revealed from heaven against all ungodliness and unrighteousness of men, who hold the truth in unrighteousness; 19 Because that which may be known of God is manifest in them; for God hath shewed it unto them. 20 For the invisible things of him from the creation of the world are clearly seen, being understood by the things that are made, even his eternal power and

Godhead; so that they are without excuse... 2 Bless the LORD, O my soul, and forget not all his benefits: 3 Who forgiveth all thineiniquities; who healeth all thy diseases; 4 Who redeemeth thy life from destruction; who crowneth thee with lovingkindness and tender mercies; 5 Who satisfieth thy mouth with good things; so that thy youth is renewed like the eagle's."

Perhaps the greatest challenge we face as human beings is that there is so much to know about God & we can never really learn too much about Him. We must even be careful so that we are not overwhelmed by His knowledge & we get lost in our effort at trying to know Him!

Back to our question: Who is God? In Gen 17:1, He introduced Himself to one of His friends, the man Abraham. Hear Him: *"When Abram was ninety-nine years old, The LORD appeared to Abram and said to him, I am Almighty God; walk before Me and be blameless."*

The word 'Almighty' here is said to mean 'El Shaddai' or 'the All-Sufficient One'. This means that inside of Him is the absolute power, ability & abundant resources to carry out all He loves & desires or determines to do. That is why any one in his/her right senses should befriend this great God. He is all that a man needs to succeed in life. We read respectively in Psalm 127:1; John 15:5; & Gen 39:2-5:

"Except the LORD build the house, they labour in vain

that build it: except the LORD keep the city, the watchman waketh but in vain...5 I am the vine, ye are the branches: He that abideth in me, and I in him, the same bringeth forth much fruit: for without me ye can do nothing... 2 And the LORD was with Joseph, and he was a prosperous man; and he was in the house of his master the Egyptian. 3 And his master saw that the LORD was with him, and that the LORD made all that he did to prosper in his hand. 4 And Joseph found grace inhis sight, and he served him: and he made him overseer over his house, and all that he had he put into his hand. 5 And it came to pass from the time that he had made him overseer in his house, and over all that he had, that the LORD blessed the Egyptian's house for Joseph's sake; and the blessing of the LORD was upon all that he had in the house, and in the field."

God is also sovereign. This means that He can do anything, use any one or anything, anywhere to achieve His purpose (see Gen 18:13-14; Psalm 115:3; Dan 4:32-35; Luke 1:37).

He can use men (even Lepers). He can use Angels, wind, rain, sunshine, fire, noise, an Ass, and even tiny insects!

Furthermore, God is Omnipotent. He is Omniscient, & Omnipresent. These mean that He has all powers, He is all-knowing, and He is ever-present. God knows you, He knows all your needs, & He has enough power to intervene. He is with you right where you are. Such knowledge should allay your fears, & also keep you from evil (Rev 1:8, 18).

The involvement of God with man started far far before we were conceived or born into this world (Jer 1:4-5, 29:11; Psalm 139:13-16). This means you are not where you are by accident! God designed it, & it is for a purpose. May you discover & fulfill your purpose in Jesus Name.

A great man of God gave a testimony of his life: He had a big problem & had tried all he knew how to. Yet there was no solution. Then someone, an uncle of his, introduced him to a church. There, he gave his life to Jesus, & a few years later he was ordained a Pastor. As fate would have it, about 8 years after his ordination, he was chosen to head the church which today has branches in most countries of the world. In other words, the problem that took him to the church & ultimately to Jesus, was a positive tool in God'shands. May God use that which you are going through at present to bring you to your destiny in Jesus Name.

In II Kings 5:1-20, the Bible tells us the story of Naaman, a Syrian Army General. Though the Bible did not tell us for how long Naaman had his skin problem, nonetheless, God used it to connect him with Himself. The Almighty God is never a loser. Rom 8:28 says:

"And we know that all things work together for good to them that love God, to them who are the called according to his purpose."

If this is true, it certainly must first work together for God Himself. This means if you are on His side, you can never be a loser.

In Gen 28:10-18, Jacob was on a journey, & the sun began to set. Then came the night, & tiredly, Jacob slept using a stone as a pillow. In his sleep, he had a dream in which he saw a ladder linking Heaven with the Earth. He also saw Angels going up & down on the ladder. In addition, Jacob also noted that God was at the top of the ladder. Then God began to speak to him. God made several promises to Jacob. One of them (Vs 15), was that Jacob would not die until He (God) had done all He promised him. I want to prophesy to you even as you are reading this: In the mighty Name of Jesus, you will not die prematurely. You will fulfill God's purpose & plan for your life (see Psalm 118:17). Are there some things you are believing God for? Is it in the area of your health, fruit of the womb, promotion, your academics or career? victory will be yours in Jesus Name. May be your concern is who to settle down with as a life partner. Whatever it is, may God step into your case & give you multiple testimonies in Jesus Name. Luke 1:36-37 says:

"36 And, behold, thy cousin Elisabeth, she hath also conceived a son in her old age: and this is the sixthmonth with her, who was called barren. For with God nothing shall be impossible."

Perhaps your spiritual life has been giving you some concern. Temptations, spiritual attacks & weariness are becoming more common to you than before, I pray that the Almighty Himself will defend and deliver you from all the forces working against your spiritual progress (see Psalm 91:1-2,9-10).

Now, Isa 59:1-2 says

"God's hands are not short that they cannot save. Nor His ears heavy that they will not hear, but your sins have created a barrier & separated you from Him, that He will not hear you".

The Bible also says in Prov 28:13 & Isa 55:6-7:

"13 He that covereth his sins shall not prosper: but whoso confesseth and forsaketh them shall have mercy....6 Seek ye the LORD while he may be found, call ye upon him while he is near: 7 Let the wicked forsake his way, and the unrighteous man his thoughts: and let him return unto the LORD, and he will have mercy upon him; and to our God, for he will abundantly pardon." There is need to acknowledge your wrongs & ask ask Him for forgiveness.

As you do, even right now, may He extend His hand of mercy to you & forgive you in Jesus Name.

Our God is a very plain & straightforward God. He is the light - the original Light, & the Father of lights. Science tells us that one of the characteristics of light is that it travels in straight lines. Light is not crooked or wobbling. I John 1:5-9 says:

"5 This then is the message which we have heard of him, and declare unto you, that God is light, and in him is no darkness at all. 6 If we say that we have fellowship with him, and walk in darkness, we lie, and do not the truth: 7 But if we walk in the light, as he is in the light, we have fellowship one with another, and the blood of Jesus Christ his Son cleanseth us from all sin. 8 If we say that we have no sin, we deceive ourselves, and the truth is not in us. 9 If we confess our sins, he is faithful and just to forgive us our sins, and to cleanse us from all unrighteousness."

It does not bend or chases an object. Any object which wants to be reflected upon or benefit from the Rays of light must come into its path! In the same manner, God's formulae are straight forward. His formulae are however very unique & peculiar. Perhaps one can add here that God's formulae is opposite that of man which is essentially rational & a kind of 'see-believe'. All a man needs is just to follow God's principles. It does not matter where you are located in this universe, it will work for you (Acts 10:34-35). The man Joseph is a classical example of this. In Gen 39:21-23; Gen 45:1-8; Gen 50:20), the Bible records that this young man Joseph feared God while at home & when eventually he found himself alone in a foreign land.

Consequently, God did not allow all the evils planned against him to succeed. As God help you to live right & fear Him, every evil that men had planned against you shall fail in Jesus Name! (See also Psalm 98:22-24).

The formulae of God simply refers to the operation or application of God's principles. God's principles are different from man's. In fact, in many cases, it is opposite of man's.

We can see all this across the Bible. For example, in Gen 26:1-3, 12-14, God told the man Isaac to remain where he was, at a time of famine. The man also sowed & in the same year he reaped a hundred fold.

Also, in Exod 15:22-25, the Israelites - God's own covenant people, had problem finding drinkable water. It may be alittle hard to understand the extent of their predicament until one realizes the dry, & rocky topography, as well as the huge population travelling at that time. In such a circumstance, there must have bee a desperate need for water. Hence the cry for water, & even an attempt at stoning Moses - their great leader! Here, God - the One whose ways are from man's, stepped in & changed the bitter water & made it drinkable. In IIKings 2:19-21 we find another example. Historically & ordinarily, the city of Jericho was beautiful - with shinning lights, well-paved roads & skyscrapers, etc. However, there were several troubles that were not so obvious. For instance, the whole city had to import water as well as food because their water was poisonous & bringing death to all - both man & animals (see also II Kgs 6:1-7; Mal 3:8-12; Lk 6:38). Often, men quarrel with IJohn 1:7-9, and argue: 'how can the blood of one man shed well over 2,000 years ago wash all men's sins away?'. Humanly speaking, that does not sound reasonable! Thank God, His ways are higher than ours (see Matt 6:4; Lk 16:15; I Sam 16:7; Isa 55:8-9).

Earlier in this chapter, I told you that a formula can be an equation. Let us look at one of God's formula: **F + O = B**. Here, F=> Fear of God; O=> Obedience; B=> Blessings.

What does it mean to **fear** God? See Prov 8:13; Psalm 128:1-2. Also, what exactly does it mean to **obey** God? Simply put, obedience means doing what God says, even when it sounds foolish or one cannot understand the reasons for it. (see Gen 22:1-18; Luke 5:5-9; ICor 1:25).

Sometime ago, my wife heard God spoke to her: "Cross over & buy a roasted corn'! Initially she argued "Lord, You know I am fasting". Thank God that she eventually obeyed. Right at the very spot where she stood a few

35

minutes earlier, there was a terrible accident that claimed 2 lives!

'Blessings', on the other hand, refers to an addition or multiplication that is far beyond what any human efforts can produce or bring (see Psalm 1:1-3; Psalm 112:1-10; Psalm 128:2-6).

The following are just a few examples of people who knew God's formulae, applied them, & the results they got:

The man Abraham - The basis of his faith & confidence in God is the integrity of God & His word. Hear him in Romans 4:17-21:

"17 (As it is written, I have made thee a father of many nations,) before him whom he believed, even God, who quickeneth the dead, and calleth those things which be not as though they were. 18 Who against hope believed in hope, that he might become the father of many nations; according to that which was spoken, So shall thy seed be. 19 And being not weak in faith, he considered not his own body now dead, when he was about an hundred years old, neither yet the deadness of Sarah's womb: 20 He staggered not at the promise of God through unbelief; but was strong in faith, giving glory to God; 21 And being fully persuaded that, what he had promised, he was able also to perform." See also Gen 22:11-18).

The Almighty Formulae

The man Isaac - Taking cue from his father Abraham, he too heard & Stuck to His instruction to remain in the land in spite of the on-going famine & economic depression. Isaac did not only remained in the land, he also invested in it - this is a further act of faith in the God who told him to stay put. I perceive that Isaac felt if God asked him not to leave, HE (God), must definitely have something positive in store!:

"19 If ye be willing and obedient, ye shall eat the good of the land....10 Say ye to the righteous, that it shall be well with him: for they shall eat the fruit of their doings

38 Now the just shall live by faith: but if any man draw back, my soul shall have no pleasure in him. (Gen 26:1-3, 12-14). Dear Reader, God has something good in stock for you - right where you are! Joseph is another example. He feared God & lived right (by not joining evil - both when at home, & when he found himself in a foreign land, far away from home. Consequently, no man could stop God's plan for his life. As you too remain obedient to God's voice, no man shall succeed in delaying or derailing your destiny in Jesus Name. Concerning Joseph, the Bible has these to say:

"5 And Joseph dreamed a dream, and he told it his brethren: and they hated him yet the more. 6 And he said unto them, Hear, I pray you, this dream which I have dreamed: 7 For, behold, we were binding sheaves in the

field, and, lo, my sheaf arose, and also stood upright; and, behold, your sheaves stood round about, and made obeisance to my sheaf. 8 And his brethren said to him, Shalt thou indeed reign over us? or shalt thou indeed have dominion over us? And they hated him yet the more for his dreams, and for his words. 9 And he dreamed yet another dream, and told it his brethren, and said, Behold, I have dreamed a dream more; and, behold, the sun and the moon and the eleven stars made obeisance to me... 2 And the LORD was with Joseph, and he was a prosperous man; and he was in the house of his master the Egyptian. 3 And his master saw that the LORD was with him, and that the LORD made all that he did to prosper in his hand. 4 And Joseph found grace in his sight, and he served him: and he made him overseer over his house, and all that he had he put into his hand. 5 And it came to pass from the time that he had made him overseer in his house, and over all that he had, that the LORD blessed the Egyptian's house for Joseph's sake; and the blessing of the LORD was upon all that he had in the house, and in the field...7 And it came to pass after these things, that his master's wife cast her eyes upon Joseph; and she said, Lie with me. 8 But he refused, and said unto his master's wife, Behold, my master wotteth not what is with me in the house, and he hath committed all that he hath to my hand; 9 There is none greater in thishouse than I; neither hath he kept back any thing from me but thee, because thou art his wife: how then can I do this great wickedness, and sin against God?... 1

Then Joseph could not refrain himself before all them that stood by him; and he cried, Cause every man to go out from me. And there stood no man with him, while Joseph made himself known unto his brethren. 2 And he wept aloud: and the Egyptians and the house of Pharaoh heard. 3 And Joseph said unto his brethren, I am Joseph; doth my father yet live? And his brethren could not answer him; for they were troubled at his presence. 4 And Joseph said unto his brethren, Come near to me, I pray you. And they came near. And he said, I am Joseph your brother, whom ye sold into Egypt. 5 Now therefore be not grieved, nor angry with yourselves, that ye sold me hither: for God did send me before you to preserve life. 6 For these two years hath the famine been in the land: and yet there are five years, in the which there shall neither be earing nor harvest. 7 And God sent me before you to preserve you a posterity in the earth, and to save your lives by a great deliverance. 8 So now it was not you that sent me hither, but God: and he hath made me a father to Pharaoh, and lord of all his house, and a ruler throughout all the land of Egypt." (Gen 37:5-9; Gen 39:2-5; 7-9; Gen 45:1-8).

Finally, we look at David. In I Sam 16:11-13, we see him arrived home to meet the man of God, Samuel, his father, Jesse, & his seven senior Brothers - all standing on their feet - apparently awaiting David's arrival & what was to happen next. Suddenly, Prophet Samuel with the Horn of oil in his right hand, moved towards David, embraced him, & began to pour oil on David's head non stop till he emptied all on him. Then Prophet Samuel loudly declared: "Today, 8th day of the Year 2015, I Prophet Samuel Elkannah in the Name of Jehohvah Elohim, the God of Israel proclaim you the next King of Israel. May the Lord God back you up, prolong your reign, & use you to subdue all the enemies of God's people, Israel". After this he, Prophet Samuelquickly packed all his baggage & departed for his base at Ramah. I believe David's Brothers, his father, & probably he too would think they were dreaming or watching a Drama. But it is real. Levels had changed, the last had become the first & the firsts had become the last! Because David had been diligent & faithful in little, God had enthroned him. BLESSINGS ALWAYS FOLLOW OBEDIENCE! God Himself said about David, in II Samuel 7:8-9:

"8 Now therefore so shalt thou say unto my servant David, Thus saith the LORD of hosts, I took thee from the sheepcote, from following the sheep, to be ruler over my people, over Israel: 9 And I was with thee whithersoever thou wentest, and have cut off all thine enemies out of thy sight, and have made thee a great name, like unto the name of the great men that are in the earth."

Have you busied yourself with praying for blessings rather than grace to obey? It is high time you change your prayers.

CHAPTER 5

THE WIND OF CHANGE
(John 3:1-8)

In John 3:1-8, we find the story of a great man called Nicodemus (a Ruler of the Jews). He came to our Lord Jesus by night. Apparently it was to come & commend or compliment Jesus for all the great things God was doing through Him. Without any doubt, Our Lord must have thanked him. BUT He was not carried away by man's accolade or the praise of men. Jesus knew that men could shout "Hosannah" today & "crucify Him" tomorrow! (See John 2:23-25).

So, Jesus went straight to tell the man Nicodemus the most important thing he needed to hear & do. As you go through this book, & especially this Chapter, may the Holy Spirit say to you & also help you to do the most important thing you need to in Jesus Name (Amen).

The most important thing that the man (Nicodemus) needed is Salvation or being Born Again. The term 'Born Again' has been misconstrued, misinterpreted & in fact taken for granted by many in our generation!

The Almighty Formulae

When chain smokers reduce their number of sticks, or drunks the number of bottles, and womanizers the numberof females they hop with, they all claim to have been 'born again'! Matt 7:21-23 says:

"21 Not every one that saith unto me, Lord, Lord, shall enter into the kingdom of heaven; but he that doeth the will of my Father which is in heaven. 22 Many will say to me in that day, Lord, Lord, have we not prophesied in thy name? and in thy name have cast out devils? and in thy name done many wonderful works? 23 And then will I profess unto them, I never knew you: depart from me, ye that work iniquity."

The Bible made it quite clear what it means to be genuinely Born Again, & why it is a must for all men. The following scriptures explain the subject in sequence:

"23 For all have sinned, and come short of the glory of God...For the wages of sin is death; but the gift of God is eternal life through Jesus Christ our Lord...He that covereth his sins shall not prosper: but whoso confesseth and forsaketh them shall have mercy...

Neither is there salvation in any other: for there is none other name under heaven given among men, whereby we must be saved." (Rom 3:23; Rom 6:23; Prov 28:13; Acts 4:12).

To be born again is far far beyond religion. It also goes beyond just going to a place of worship. It is a spiritual experience that involves being made free from sin & it's consequences. When sins are confessed from the heart, & genuinely repented of, the mercy promised by God begins to flow. The repentant heart is made right with God. This brings peace of mind Romans 5:1; 8:1-2 state it this way: *"Therefore being justified by faith, we have peace with God through our Lord Jesus Christ...There is therefore now no condemnation to them which are in Christ Jesus, who walk not after the flesh, but after the Spirit. For the law of the Spirit of life in Christ Jesus hath made me free from the law of sin and death."*

The response of Nicodemus (in Vs 4 of John), reveals that a man could be highly placed in the physical, the secular, or even in the intellectual world & yet be seriously ignorant of spiritual things. It also shows that a man could be high in religious circles & still be ignorant of things that matter in eternity - both to God & to man! Hence, in John 8:32, our Lord Jesus said:

"And ye shall know the truth, and the truth will set you free".

One of the characteristics of the wind is that it is invisible, it can not be seen! Also, it cannot be held. Yet, we all feel & experience its presence, it's power & actions. I told some people somewhere that even though wind is invisible, yet, it appears that it has eyes & can see. It also has hands & can carry objects from one place to another. It may also have mouth since it speaks, make noise & even whistles!

Some winds can cause great devastation. For instance, Hurricane, Tsunami, Typhoon, etc.

The word "CHANGE" is a very important concept or phenomenon. It involves a movement from one point or stage to another. Change can be positive or negative. It can also be for good or for evil. Change can be upwards or downwards. It could be forward or backwards. For example, when the sick gets healed, or the barren becomes a mother. Also, when the unemployed get a good job, or the poor becomes rich & wealthy. All these are positive changes. On the other hand, when someone who used to be healthy suddenly becomes sick, or the rich becomes poor, or the employed gets sacked, and so on, then we are talking about negative changes. I pray for you dear Reader, that your change will always be positive, upwards, & forward &

In Jesus Name. I pray same for myself too! May we never again experience negative changes in Jesus Name.

Perhaps you recently had a dream & you found yourself in a reverse gear, & you were moving fast backwards! I decree in the Mighty Name of Jesus that all the plans of the enemy to retard or reverse your progress & destiny shall be cancelled in Jesus Name (Amen).

As there is a physical wind, so there is a spiritual wind. The spiritual wind is far more powerful than the physical wind.

In the Bible, one of the symbols used to represent or describe the Holy Spirit, is the wind. So, when we talk about the Wind of Change, we are in fact referring to the Holy Spirit. The Holy Spirit is the wind of change! We cannot see Him, we cannot hold Him. Yet He is very real & very powerful. John 3: 5-8 says:

"5 Jesus answered, Verily, verily, I say unto thee, Except a man be born of water and of the Spirit, he cannot enter into the kingdom of God. 6 That which is born of the flesh is flesh; and that which is born of the Spirit is spirit. 7 Marvel not that I said unto thee, Ye must be born again. 8 The wind bloweth where it listeth, and thou hearest the sound thereof, but canst not tell whence it cometh, and whither it goeth: so is every one that is born of the Spirit."

As the Wind of Change, the Holy Spirit can do many great & wonderful things - things that no other power can do (Zac 4:6-7). For instance, the Holy Spirit can make ways where there was none. That was what happened at the parting of the Red Sea. God blew the wind over the Red

Sea, & ways appeared for His children (see Exod 14:13-22). May God cause ways to open for you in Jesus Name. In Acts 12:5-11, the Bible gave a vivid account of how the man, Peter was supernaturally released from prison. Here, God caused a spiritual wind to blow in answer to the prayers of some of His children. It led to Peter being ushered out of prison where he had been kept, awaiting execution. Are you surrounded by prison walls, or chained & restricted? The wind of the Holy Spirit will blow & break all restrictions & obstacles on your way in Jesus Name.

As the Wind of Change, the Holy Spirit can open the womb of the barren. Some years back, the Lord brought me in contact with a young woman. She was the wife of Minister of God. They had been married for close to seven years but had no children. Discovering this, I invited her for that year's Holy Ghost Service at the Redemption Camp (Lagos, Nigeria). God visited her at the Programme. Less than a year later, this woman was already carrying a Baby boy in her hands! May be you too are believing God for a miracle like this - either directly for yourself, your children, or a loved one. God will answer you in Jesus Name.

As The Wind of Change, the Holy Spirit can make the lame walk (Acts 3: 2-9). As the Wind of change, the Holy Spirit can raise the dead (Ezek 37: 1-10; Rom 8:11). As the Wind of Change, the Holy Spirit can take a man from point A to point B (Acts 8:26-40). By God's grace, I am what & where I am today, because of a word I got from the Holy Spirit years ago - while a student at the University of Birmingham, UK. That word led to my decision to become a full-time Missionary. That word moved (is still moving) me even till today! May you too hear from the Holy Spirit today & may God help you to be obedient in Jesus Name. I PERCEIVE HE HAS ALREADY BEEN SPEAKING TO YOU! On the other hand & when the need arises, the Holy Spirit as a wind of change can also do some apparently dangerous & terrible things. For example, He can make the one who sees to become blind (II Kings 6:16-24; Acts

13:4-12). He can kill intruders or hypocrites (Acts 5:1-11; Job 5:12). I don't know in what area of your life you need the Wind of Change to blow & bring positive changes. Is it in your body, your health, your marriage, your finances? Or is it in your spiritual life? May God send His Wind into your life in Jesus Name.

Is there anything a person needs to do to ensure that the Wind of Change blows positively in his or her direction? The answer is Yes! For the wind to blow & do you good, you must rightly position yourself. In Exod 32, Moses wanted to command the wind to blow & he remembered that when the wind first blew by the Red Sea, it had a positive effect for God's children, & a negative effect on their enemies. So, in verse 26, he asked the Question: *"Who*

is on the Lord's side?" The Bible said only the Sons of Levi answered him. On whose side are you - the Lord's side or the enemy's?

You may want to pray as follows:

Father, thank You for Your Word, thank You for speaking to my life.

Father, let Your wind blow for me & give me a positve change - let it be a wind of healing, deliverance, victory, etc. Father, let Your wind blow & make a way for me where there was none.

Father, let Your wind of favour blow towards me & accelerate my progress, promotion & destiny.

Father, let Your wind blow away every hindrance & obstacle to my destiny.

Holy Spirit, You are the Spirit of wisdom, knowledge, understanding, Might & Counsel. Please blow over my life & give me wisdom, knowledge, & understanding. Holy Spirit, be my Helper.

Also, please join me to Pray for the "Nicodemuses" of our generation - those people who are big & highly placed, but who are highly ignorant of things that matter in eternity.

Many of them are in govt - as Mayors, Kings, Presidents, Prime Ministers, Professionals, etc; Governors, Business Executives, they are also in religious circles as Church, Ministry or denominational leaders. Ask God to open their eyes of understanding so they can see & be converted to Jesus.

CHAPTER 6

THE UNTOUCHABLES
(II Tim 2:15-21; Psalm 105:14-15)

When something is said to be "untouchable", it means it is a no-go area. It is forbidden. Going near or touching it can have a lot of grave consequences. The same applies when we say that someone is untouchable. If you maltreat or exploit such a man or woman, you will be in for it!

In Gen 2:15-17, the Bible records a one-to-one discussion between God & Adam (the first created man):

"Then the Lord God took the man and put him in the Garden of Eden to tend and to keep it. And the Lord commanded the man, saying, 'Of every tree of the garden you may freely eat; But of the tree of the knowledge of good and evil you shall not eat, for in the day that you eat of it you shall surely die."

For God's true children, some things are untouchables. To think of or go near them will be an indication that such a child of God is looking for trouble!

The Almighty Formulae

The first and most critical among the untouchables is SIN! In II Tim 2:19, the Bible says: *"Nevertheless the solid foundation of God stands sure, having this seal: the Lord knows those who are His own, Let everyone who names the Name of the Lord depart from iniquity"*

Ephesians 5: 1-8 expressly lists some specific sins, and went on to declare that they should not even be mentioned in the midst of God's true children:

"1 Be ye therefore followers of God, as dear children; 2 And walk in love, as Christ also hath loved us, and hath given himself for us an offering and a sacrifice to God for a sweetsmelling savour. 3 But fornication, and all uncleanness, or covetousness, let it not be once named among you, as becometh saints; 4 Neither filthiness, nor foolish talking, nor jesting, which are not convenient: but rather giving of thanks. 5 For this ye know, that no whoremonger, nor unclean person, nor covetous man, who is an idolater, hath any inheritance in the kingdom of Christ and of God. 6 Let no man deceive you with vain words: for because of these things cometh the wrath of God upon the children of disobedience. 7 Be not ye therefore partakers with them. 8 For ye were sometimes darkness, but now are ye light in the Lord: walk as children of light:"

In the generation we are today, not only are these evils common among many of God's children & Christians, but in many churches, they are even celebrated. Worse still, they are becoming the order of the day among so called Ministers. In Luke 16:15, Jesus accused the Pharisees:

"15 And he said unto them, Ye are they which justify yourselves before men; but God knoweth your hearts: for that which is highly esteemed among men is abomination in the sight of God."

No wonder, Apostle Peter said in I Peter 4: 17:

"For the time has come for judgment to begin at the house of God, and if it begins with us first, what will be the end of those who do not obey the gospel of God?" Malachi 3:6 says:

"For I am the LORD, I do not change; Therefore you are not consumed O sons of Jacob".

Often, when we are desperate for a miracle, we quote this very passage of the Scriptures. However, this verse is more true in relation to the character of God than in relation to His power. God's character & integrity determine to a very great extent, His power & the exercise of it! Our God has not changed in His character. He is still holy today as He was in eternity past. His hatred & zero tolerance for sin has not changed:

"21 Though hand join in hand, the wicked shall not be

unpunished: but the seed of the righteous shall be delivered. 22 As a jewel of gold in a swine's snout, so is a fair woman which is without discretion. 23 The desire of the righteous is only good: but the expectation of the wicked is wrath... 7 But the heavens and the earth, which are now, by the same word are kept in store, reserved unto fire against the day of judgment and perdition of ungodly men. 8 But, beloved, be not ignorant of this one thing, that one day is with the Lord as a thousand years, and a thousand years as one day. 9 The Lord is not slack concerning his promise, as some men count slackness; but is longsuffering to us- ward, not willing that any should perish, but that all should come to repentance." (Prov 11:21,23; II Peter

3:7-9).

May His mercy & patience never expire over your life & mine in Jesus Name (see Prov 1:24-33). Second among the 'Untouchables' is Tithes - a tenth of every man's income. God requires that this should voluntarily be released to Him. The reason is very clear: IT RIGHTFULLY BELONGS TO HIM! Malachi 3:8-12 declares:

"8 Will a man rob God? Yet ye have robbed me. But ye say, Wherein have we robbed thee? In tithes and offerings. 9 Ye are cursed with a curse: for ye have robbed me, even this whole nation. 10 Bring ye all the tithes into the

storehouse, that there may be meat in mine house, and prove me now herewith, saith the LORD of hosts, if I will not open you the windows of heaven, and pour you out a blessing, that there shall not be room enough to receive it. 11 And I will rebuke the devourer for your sakes, and he shall not destroy the fruits of your ground; neither shall your vine cast her fruit before the time in the field, saith the LORD of hosts. 12 And all nations shall call you blessed: for ye shall be a delightsome land, saith the LORD of hosts."

Any one who spends, eats, or steals Tithes, is under a curse. A curse has been defined as 'a summon to forces in heaven, on earth, & underneath the earth - visible & invisible, to work against somebody'. Curses are very dangerous because when it is at work, it affects everything & whatsoever is connected with the one under such a curse. Anywhere he goes, anything he touches, & anyone who associates with him will have a taste of it (see Gen 20:1-18; Joshua 7:10-26; II Kings 2:19-21).

Third among the 'Untouchables', is the glory of God. Isa 42:8 says:

"8 I am the LORD: that is my name: and my glory will I not give to another, neither my praise to graven images."

The Fourth 'Untouchable' is God's very owned children, especially His true Ministers. The Bible called the former 'the Apple of His eyes', & the latter, His 'Anointed ones' (Deut 32:10; Zechariah 2:8; Psalm 105:14-15). From the Scriptures, it is clear that even Kings who joked with or took God's children & Servants for granted & maltreated them did not go scot-free!

The plan of God is to make you & me, as well as everything connected with us untouchable to the enemy (Deut 32:10; Zac 2:8). This will happen only & only if we too stay clear of the things which God Himself declared as 'Untouchables'.

When we obey God's word & stay clear of what He forbids, then we too will become a 'No-go' area for Satan & his cohorts.

All across the Scriptures, we see God honoring His word to make His children & Servants truly untouchable (see Exod 8:22-23; Exod 9:3-7; Exod 9:23-26; Num 32:20-23; Psalm 105:14-15; Isa 54:17; Isa 43:4-6; Isa 63:8-10). Today, even in our generation, that same God is still creating a line of demarcation between His true children & Ministers on the one hand, and those who are not His own, on the other.

I once heard of the story of how God spared the house of an old & very elderly Christian somewhere in the central part of the USA. There was three days of continuous strong & devastating wind. She came out on the fourth morning to see the extensive damage in the neighbourhood with her 4- bedroom bungalow as the only building still standing!

Fire broke out in high density area of a West African city sometime ago. This strange fire raced down houses No 1,3, & 5. It jumped over house No 7, and continued its destructive work at house No 9, 11, 13, etc, before theGovernment Fire Brigade came to put it off. I pray that on the day when evil is at work to kill, maim, & waste lives or properties, the Lord will create a line of demarcation between you & all evil in Jesus Name.

In some areas of our work in the mission fields, we have seen God dramatically making us truly untouchable to Satan & all his allies. In June 1994, early on a Monday morning, somewhere in an East African city, an elderly man came in with a young man. After a long & somehow boring story and deep apologies 'for all we did to you since you came to us', this elderly man asked the young man (who I understood later to be a pastor from another Church), to please join him to ask me for forgiveness. Up till today, I can not actually pinpoint what they did! However, I perceive if an elderly man came that early morning & began to beg a small boy like me, it's most like they had done a little of something! Great thanks to God. He said in Isa 54:17 & Psalm 89:22-24:

"17 No weapon that is formed against thee shall prosper; and every tongue that shall rise against thee in judgment thou shalt condemn. This is the heritage of the servants of the LORD, and their righteousness is of me, saith the

The Almighty Formulae

LORD...22 The enemy shall not exact upon him; nor the son of wickedness afflict him. 23 And I will beat down his foes before his face, and plague them that hate him. 24 But my faithfulness and my mercy shall be with him: and in my name shall his horn be exalted."

Not very long ago, I was in an official car travelling on an express/freeway. There was a little traffic hold up & the traffic was slow. Suddenly our Driver (who, thank God, was spirit filled), swerved & joined an external lane, even though it appeared the line we left was moving faster. As I opened my mouth and about to ask why he changed lane, we heard a continuous crashing in of series of vehicles on the lane we were on just a little before! About 8-10 vehicles were involved. We later realized that the brakes of a Petrol Tanker had failed. So, the Tanker just carried every vehicle in its way, starting with the one immediately behind us on the former lane!

By God's grace, I worked in the public Service before the Lord called me to full-time ministry. For a period of ten solid years, & while some of my colleagues were posted from one Ministry/Department to another (some, up to three or four times), I was left in one Department! All the promotions & in-service training I was due for, met me in that same Department. It was after I became a full-minister, that I began to realize that God made me 'untouchable' because He knew I would need the long experience of that Department when eventually I answered His call (Rev 1:18). God did the same with people like Jeremiah & Daniel in foreign lands.

To be untouchable, your life must please God. In Acts 10:34-35, the Bible says:

"34 Then Peter opened his mouth, and said, Of a truth I perceive that God is no respecter of persons: 35 But in every nation he that feareth him, and worketh righteousness, is accepted with him."

Put in another way, this text tells us that anyone who fears God & does what is right before Him, will become untouchable. When they are sacking or terminating others, in his/her place of work, his/her name will not be on the list. When evil is passing, it won't come near him/her. If it is ahead of him/her, he/she will not reach it. If it is behind, it will not overtake him/her. Exodus 12:12-13 declares:

"12 For I will pass through the land of Egypt this night, and will smite all the firstborn in the land of Egypt, both man and beast; and against all the gods of Egypt I will execute judgment: I am the LORD. 13 And the blood shall be to you for a token upon the houses where ye are: and when I see the blood, I will pass over you, and the plague shall not be upon you to destroy you, when I smite the land of Egypt." (See also Psalm 91:1-2,9-10).

Finally, the question arises: On whose side are you - on the Lord's side or on the Devil's side? In Exod 12:12-13 quoted earlier, it is clear that the Blood worked or protected those who were in the houses that bore the Blood on its door. It means if the Blood has not washed you, it can not protect you (see Rom 6:1-2; Isa 55:6-7; I John 1:5-7). You may want to pray as follows:

• Father, anything the enemy can point at in my life & use to accuse or afflict me, please forgive me totally.

• Father, please make me pure & holy. Don't let me touch anything untouchable.

• Father, make me & my family untouchable to evil, Satan, & dangers.

• Father, let there be a clear demarcation between me and evil.

• Father, let there be a marked difference between me and the unbelievers.

• Father, everywhere I go, let Your glory be seen in me.

• Father, give joy to all who are weeping in secret (Psalm 30:5).

CHAPTER 7

"THE MAN CALLED SIMON"
(Acts 8:4-13)

The Text above is on a man called Simon the Sorcerer. He held the whole City of Samaria asway, & kept everyone in bondage & fear!

Thank God one day, light came. Another man, Philip - an Evangelist, a Holy Ghost carrier, entered Samaria & he made a great difference. Let us look at some lessons from the Text.

Wherever darkness reigns, people will be in serious trouble. In this City of Samaria, people had several problems. In the main, these could be traced to Simon. Many may have seen him as a solution. But in reality he was a cause. He must have bewitched some, cast spells on some, & enchanted the people. Through his evil disciples, advertisers, or agents, he would have greatly promoted his evil trade. Numbers 23:23 says:

"Surely there is no enchantment against Jacob, neither is there any divination against Israel: according to this time

it shall be said of Jacob and of Israel, What hath God wrought!"

It is very important to be extra careful who you associate with & where you go for help. Also be watchful also who you take advice or counsel from.

"Be not deceived: evil communications corrupt good manners... Blessed is the man that walketh not in the counsel of the ungodly, nor standeth in the way of sinners, nor sitteth in the seat of the scornful." (I Cor 15:33; Psalm 1:1).

The truth is that Satan does not give anything free of charge. The Lord Jesus said in John 10:10,"The thief cometh not, but for to steal, and to kill, and to destroy: I am come that they might have life, and that they might have it more abundantly. I Peter 5:8-9 adds:

"8 Be sober, be vigilant; because your adversary the devil, as a roaring lion, walketh about, seeking whom he may devour: 9 Whom resist stedfast in the faith, knowing that the same afflictions are accomplished in your brethren that are in the world." (See also I John 3:7-10).

Any need that God cannot or does not meet, & any problem God can not or does not solve obviously has no other solution somewhere else. We thank God for His awesome & unlimited power, for no situation is beyond

"The Man Called Simon"

Him. He can solve any problem, heal any disease, no matter it's source, or for how long it has existed (Mal 3:6; Exod 15:26; Luke 1:37).

This human principality over the City & Region of Samaria - the man Simon the Sorcerer - was feared by everybody, both great & small. He can easily be referred to or called a negative 'critical person'!

Who is a 'Critical person'? He/she is a man or woman who has a great influence (positively or negatively) in a place. When you enter a territory - be it an office, an organization, a city, a nation, or even a church, watch out for such people. In every place, there is always at least one critical person - either negatively or positively. You will need to prayerfully identify him/her (or them). You must ask God to open your eyes to recognize them. If negative, you will need to put him or her under 'spiritual surveillance'. This is so that he or she does not continue to hinder God's Kingdom work, or waste your own destiny. On the other hand, if positive, you must ask God to connect you with them - because they can be a very useful force in helping you fulfill your purpose & destiny. For example, in the book of Esther, at least three critical persons were mentioned - Mordecai & Esther on the positive side, & the man Haman on the other (see Esther 3:6-15; 6:11-13; 7:10).

The good thing however, is that negative critical persons

can change - God can change them. God can arrest them. Fervent & focused prayers can cripple them! (See Acts 9:1-9).

The activities & negative influence of Simon in the great City of Samaria should be of concern to us today, even in our owngeneration. Sorcery, witchcraft, magical activities, etc, have become common & legalized. It is being taught in schools from nursery through to tertiary institutions. Corporate outfits even require their staff to sign up for! Years ago, as a Missionary in an African country, a confirmed sorcerer was invited to come & 'sanctify' the national head office of a large company. Worse still, sorcery & witchcraft had creeped into the Church too. Several lying wonders are products or manifestations of enchantments, divination, sorcery, magic, etc.

Some 'special' anointing oils, soaps, rings, handkerchiefs, holy waters, etc, are from dangerous sources. Many 'fall down & die' prayers & night vigils are cover ups for all these evil & shady deeds. It is worrisome if not fearful that the same God who said in His Word (Ezek 18:23) that He is not interested in the death of Sinners is the one some of His children are calling upon to kill their fellow Christians! It appears some people have turned God's house into another thing.

Our Lord Jesus warned in Matthew 7:15-23:

"15 Beware of false prophets, which come to you in sheep's clothing, but inwardly they are ravening wolves. 16 Ye shall know them by their fruits. Do men gather grapes of thorns, or figs of thistles? 17 Even so every good tree bringeth forth good fruit; but a corrupt tree bringeth forth evil fruit. 18 A good tree cannot bring forth evil fruit, neither can a corrupt tree bring forth good fruit. 19 Every tree that bringeth not forth good fruit is hewn down, and cast into the fire. 20 Wherefore by their fruits ye shall know them. 21 Not every one that saith unto me, Lord, Lord, shall enter into the kingdom of heaven; but he that doeth the will of my Father which is in heaven. 22 Many will say to me in that day, Lord, Lord, have we not prophesied in thy name? and in thy name have cast out devils? and in thy name done many wonderful works? 23 And then will I profess unto them, I never knew you: depart from me, ye that work iniquity.".

The lessons here are many. The first is that Light, no matter how little, is superior to darkness. In Samaria, as it is also today, the entry of Light & Truth, brings men out of darkness into light, & out of deception into total freedom:

"Then spake Jesus again unto them, saying, I am the light of the world: he that followeth me shall not walk in darkness, but shall have the light of life...32 And ye shall know the truth, and the truth shall make you free. 36 If the Son therefore shall make you free, ye shall be free

indeed...Jesus saith unto him, I am the way, the truth, and the life: no man cometh unto the Father, but by me." (John 8:12, 32, 36; 14:6).

Secondly, you alone can make a difference where you are. - in your home, neighbourhood, School, Office, Church, City, Nation, etc. It is not how long darkness had been there that matters, it is the power of light that is important:

"And the light shineth in darkness; and the darkness comprehended it not."

Philip alone made a great difference in Samaria. All that he, Philip (the Evangelist) did was was to preach Christ - His Name & the Kingdom of God which Jesus brought, as well as what that Kingdom can offer anyone who chooses to come into it - Forgiveness, Salvation from sin, healing, deliverance, peace of mind, etc. What gave power & backing to the things Philip preached was the Holy Spirit. We need Him today more than ever (see Acts 1:8; Acts 10:38). It may interest you to know that God has divinely put you where you are so you can make a positive difference. May your life count for God in your generation in Jesus Name.

"1 Arise, shine; for thy light is come, and the glory of the LORD is risen upon thee. 2 For, behold, the darkness shall cover the earth, and gross darkness the people: but the LORD shall arise upon thee, and his glory shall be seen

upon thee. 3 And the Gentiles shall come to thy light, and kings to the brightness of thy rising...13 Ye are the salt of the earth: but if the salt have lost his savour, wherewith shall it be salted? it is thenceforth good for nothing, but to be cast out, and to be trodden under foot of men. 14 Ye are the light of the world. A city that is set on an hill cannot be hid. 15 Neither do men light a candle, and put it under a bushel, but on a candlestick; and it giveth light unto all that are in the house. 16 Let your light so shine before men, that they may see your good works, and glorify your Father which is in heaven...4 In him was life; and the life was the lightof men. 5 And the light shineth in darkness; and the darkness comprehended it not." (Isa 60:1-3; Matt 5:13-16; John1:4-5).

Further to the arrival of Philip, something very interesting happened agin in Samaria. The Bible says in Acts 8:13:

"And Simon too believed, and was baptized"!

Several questions can agitate one's mind here. for example, 'Why did Simon choose to believe & be baptized'? There are several possibilities. God may have genuinely touched his heart. As we said earlier, there is no negative critical person that God can not change for good. Simon may also have been fascinated, amazed & astonished by what he saw at the Crusade being conducted by (Philip the

Evangelist). Raw miracles may have caught his attention. At the mention of the Name of Jesus, the blind eyes opened, the lame stood up & started walking/running around, those that were demon possessed got their deliverances! Simon would have opened his mouth & wondered: "can this be real - no rituals, no incantations, no spells, no gymnastics?" The people he once held bound were being set free by the powerful Name of Jesus through a man as 'ordinary' as Philip! Simon, of course may have accepted Jesus for economic reasons. He may have realized that he needed to act 'fast' - since he was losing grounds. All his customers were no more patronizing him. After all it is said "if you can not beat them, join them"! Like Simon, many are in church or claim to be saved & born again today for several reasons other than serving God & making it to Heaven at the end:

"13 And the Jews' passover was at hand, and Jesus went up to Jerusalem, 14 And He found in the temple those that sold oxen and sheep and doves, and the changers of money sitting: 15 And when he had made a scourge of small cords, he drove them all out of the temple, and with the sheep, and the oxen; and poured out the changers' money, and overthrew the tables; 16 And said unto them that sold doves, Take these things hence; make not my Father's house an house of merchandise...23 Now when he was in Jerusalem at the passover, in the feast day, many believed in his name, when they saw the miracles which he did. 24

But Jesus did not commit himself unto them, because he knew all men, 25 Andneeded not that any should testify of man: for he knew what was in man." (John 2:13-16, 23-25).

May be you should ask yourself some candid questions: "WHY AM I IN CHURCH". "WHY AM I IN THE PARTICULAR DENOMINATION I AM?" WHY AM I CLAIMING TO BE A CHRISTIAN & IN KINGDOM SERVICE"? Whatever brought you to a Church or to being born again, or whatever has been driving all your actions over time, as you are reading this book, let God give you a new reason. Let your reason be to seek first the Kingdom of God & His righteousness:

"31 Therefore take no thought, saying, What shall we eat? or, What shall we drink? or, Wherewithal shall we be clothed? 32 (For after all these things do the Gentiles seek:) for your heavenly Father knoweth that ye have need of all these things. 33 But seek ye first the kingdom of God, and his righteousness; and all these things shall be added unto you. 34 Take therefore no thought for the morrow: for the morrow shall take thought for the things of itself. Sufficient unto the day is the evil thereof." Matthew 6: 31-31.

We shall conclude this chapter with a look at some things the man Simon did after his purported conversion. First he sought & got baptized. Genuine salvation is a decision to forsake evil ways of the past & start following a new way of righteousness. No one on his or her own volition can successfully take this important decision. We all need the help of the Holy Spirit. It is the Holy Spirit who convicts the heart (see Rom 10:9-14; Prov 28:13; II Cor 5:17; Rom 7:14-25). Under normal circumstances, Water baptism is a step further in the spiritual journey of a Believer. While there is no where it is written that if a man is not baptized he would be denied entry to Heaven, yet it is clear that as long as we remain in the physical body, & in this world, we need to be baptized by immersion (Acts 8:29-38).

Water Baptism by immersion is a public declaration of our new life in Christ. It signifies the death & resurrection of Jesus (Rom 6:1-6). A man living in sin can be likened to some one lost & drowned at sea. Salvation rescues him from the evil of being drowned & dying. Before this rescue, it is most likely that the man would have drank some liters of dirty water. On arriving at the shores, all the dirty water would need to be pressed out of his belly. So, while Salvation gets a man out of evil, the process of getting evil out of every man, is termed "deliverance". Today, many people are truly & genuinely saved or born again, some are even in Ministry. However, when we see their life style - their dressing, their behavior, or even the way they lobby for position, mishandle Kingdom resources, etc, we wonder if the person is actually saved & born again at all! Well, they may have. The problem is that while such people have been rescued from evil, the greater evils in them are still very intact!

Rather than go for deliverance, the man Simon opted for water Baptism, & thought everything was over! The Legion of demons he had acquired over the years, & with which he had been holding the whole city of Samaria to ransom before Philip came to town, were still alive & very active in him.

If for any reason you too are like Simon, you do some things that even you yourself know are unchristianly, but you can not help it, I advise that you humbly seek help. May the Lord totally set you free in Jesus Name, Amen (John 8: 32, 36).

CHAPTER 8

HELP ON THE WAY
(Psalm 127:1)

Every man needs help in one form or the other. This is because no one is all sufficient, only God is. It is unfortunate that some people think they don't need help. Many who realize that they need help often go to the wrong sources.

Rather than being helped, they end up with more problems. May the Holy Spirit send you the help you need in Jesus Name, Amen.

Help can be defined as 'an action taken to give assistance to someone'. That action can be in the form of a word, a song, a gift, a gesture, a prayer, a testimony, or a note or text message. The action may even be a mere silence! It should be noted that not all helps or assistance given or sent to the one in need do get to them when and where they are needed. We are living in a sophisticated world, yet something has become part of our vocabulary. We call it is "network problem"! This makes it impossible for many a help to reach the ones they are meant for. Whether physically or spiritually, I pray that network problems will not rob you of the help God intends for you in Jesus Name. This means that a true help is the assistance that comes to us when and where we need it. It is an assistance that adds value to our lives.In life, there is no one who can boldly say he or she does not need help. Everybody needs help in one form or the other. If a man says he does not need any help, it means his number one problem is that he does not know that he needs help!

Ordinarily speaking, there three basic sources of help available to every man. The first is that every man can, to some great extent, help himself. Also, men can help us.

Finally, God can help us. Let us look at each of these more closely.

As a man or woman, you can help yourself. Did you ask how? Yes, in several ways. For example, you can help yourself by doing the right things at the right time. Eccles 3:1 says:

"1 To every thing there is a season, and a time to every purpose under the heaven:"

You can also help yourself by being at the right place at the right time. Psalm 84:11 declares:

"11 For the LORD God is a sun and shield: the LORD will

give grace and glory: no good thing will he withhold from them that walk uprightly."

Furthermore, you can help yourself by moving with the right people and by taking advice from the right people In I Cor 15:33, the Bible says:

"Be not deceived: evil communications corrupt good manners."

The Contemporary English Version of the Bible makes it more apt:

"Don't fool yourselves. Bad friends will destroy you."!

Are you a young person? Let me ask you: Who are you moving with? Who do you call your friends? Are they helpers or destroyers of your destiny?

Psalm 1:1-3, & 119:63, say to you & me:

"1 Blessed is the man that walketh not in the counsel of the ungodly, nor standeth in the way of sinners, nor sitteth in the seat of the scornful.

2 But his delight is in the law of the LORD; and in his law doth he meditate day and night. 3 And he shall be like a tree planted by the rivers of water, that bringeth forth his fruit in his season; his leaf also shall not wither; and whatsoever he doeth shall prosper....I am a companion of all them that fear thee, and of them that keep thy precepts."

Men can help us. They can give us gifts, they can recommend us for appointment or promotion, etc. Friends, spouses, parents, children, relations, strangers, & even enemies can be moved by God to assist or help us. If you are a stranger or got stranded in a new place, you can ask for direction, & be helped (See Gen 37: 14-15). For example, the first car I ever owned and rode in my life was a gift. I was so unprepared for the miracle that I had to employ a Driver for over a year!

As good as personal help and help from men may be, they are highly limited. For example, you can help yourself only if you know or agree that you have a need. Many are blind to the needs in their lives. Many people who reject Jesus today do so because they are spiritually blind and they don't see the need for Him. Yet, the Bible says salvation is a must for every man, and only JESUS can save:

"23 For all have sinned, and come short of the glory of God; ...23 For the wages of sin is death; but the gift of God is eternal life through Jesus Christ our Lord 12Neither is there salvation in any other: for there is none other name under heaven given among men, whereby we must be saved...5 This then is the message which we have heard of him, and declare unto you, that God is light, and in him is

no darkness at all. 6 If we say that we have fellowship with him, and walk in darkness, we lie, and do not the truth: 7 But if we walk in the light, as he is in the light, we have fellowship one with another, and the blood of Jesus Christ his Son cleanseth us from all sin. 8 If we say that we have no sin, we deceive ourselves, and the truth is not in us. 9 If we confess our sins, he is faithful and just to forgive us our sins, and to cleanse us from all unrighteousness...20 Behold, I stand at the door, and knock: if any man hear my voice, and open the door, I will come in to him, and will sup with him, and he with me." (Rom 3:23; 6:23; Acts 4:12; I John 1: 5-9; Rev 3:20).

Also, men may not know your needs. There are times, when we cannot disclose what we are going through with men.

So, they are unaware of our needs and cannot help, unless & except God reveals it & compels them to help you. On the other hand, there are needs we have that even when some people know they won't be bothered an inch! In the vivid story in Luke 16:19-21, our Lord Jesus told the parable of the Rich man & Lazarus. The story showed clearly that men can sometimes be seriously selfish and unconcerned about you and your problems. Of course there are instances when men are limited and do not have the capacity to help us if even they care and are concerned. The case of Jacob and his wife Rachel is a classical example, in Gen 30:1-2, we read:

"1 And when Rachel saw that she bare Jacob no children, Rachel envied her sister; and said unto Jacob, Give me children, or else I die. 2 And Jacob's anger was kindled against Rachel: and he said, Am I in God's stead, who hath withheld from thee the fruit of the womb?"

Imagine a man who woke up one morning and was getting ready for work. As he was adjusting his tie in front of the mirror just before finally going out, and the wife blocked his way and grabbed him by the neck, furiously shouting "Unless you make me pregnant today, you are going nowhere!" Jacob's answer shows how concerned but helpless he was for his wife's situation. Thank God that He is not limited by what limits man. In Gen 30:22-24, the Bible says:

"And God remembered Rachel, and God hearkened to her, and opened her womb. And she conceived, and bare a son; and said, God hath taken away my reproach: And she called his name Joseph; and said, The Lord shall add to me another son".

Are you desperate for a miracle of conception? The Lord who remembered Rachel will remember you today. He will turn your mourning to dancing. While one cannot rule out the possibility that God often uses & can still use men to help us, it must be emphasized that the focus should be on God and Him God alone. In Jer 17:5-8, the Bible alerts: *"Thus saith the LORD; Cursed be the man that trusteth in man, and maketh flesh his arm, and whose heart departeth from the LORD. 6 For he shall be like the heath in the desert, and shall not see when good cometh; but shall inhabit the parched places in the wilderness, in a salt land and not inhabited. 7 Blessed is the man that trusteth in the LORD, and whose hope the LORD is. 8 For he shall be as a tree planted by the waters, and that spreadeth out her roots by the river, and shall not see when heat cometh, but her leaf shall be green; and shall not be careful in the year of drought, neither shall cease from yielding fruit."*

What are all these telling us? First, the true source of help and the only true Helper is God, and one else. Psalm 127:1 reads:

"1 Except the LORD build the house, they labour in vain that build it: except the LORD keep the city, the watchman waketh but in vain."

Here, we see what could be referred to as 2 divine equations: (i) $M-G=F$; (ii) $M+G=S$ (where M, G, F, & S refer to man, God, Failure & Success, respectively). Man without God will end up an absolute failure, because except the Lord builds the house, truly they labour in vain that build it! On the other hand, if & when a man makes God his senior partner, he will succeed tremendously. In fact, failure will become a stranger to him. Thank God that He is ever willing and waiting to help us (please see Matt 8:1-3; James 1:5; Isa 41:10-13; Jer 17:5,9).

David was a man who always sought and got God's divine assistance. In Psalms 121:1-2, he said:

"I will lift up my eyes unto the hills, from whence cometh my help. My help cometh from the Lord, who made heaven and earth" (see also Psalm 124:1-8).

How then do we get help from God, or put in other words, Who can get help from God? To be helped by God, the first thing is you must realize you need His help. Many are either ignorant of their need for help or are blinded to it. Some men think they are self-sufficient or that they know it all and can be in control. As long as a man thinks he can handle things by himself, God will fold His arms:

"5 I am the vine, ye are the branches: He that abideth in me, and I in him, the same bringeth forth much fruit: forwithout me ye can do nothing...3 Trust in the LORD, and do good; so shalt thou dwell in the land, and verily thou shalt be fed. 4 Delight thyself also in the LORD; and he shall give thee the desires of thine heart. 5 Commit thy way unto the LORD; trust also in him; and he shall bring it to pass. 6 And he shall bring forth thy righteousness as the light, and thy judgment as the noonday. 7 Rest in the LORD, and wait patiently for him: fret not thyself because

of him who prospereth in his way, because of the man who bringeth wicked devices to pass." (John 15:5; Psalm 37:3-7).

Secondly, you must call upon Him for the help you need. Now, because He is a holy God, the sin in the life of a man always hinder or create a gap in between (Isa 59:1-2; Psalm 66:18). So, for a man to be able to approach God he must first settle the question of his/her sins (Rom3:23; Isa 55:6-7; I John 1:5-9). The first call or prayer of a Sinner that God will be attentive to, is the prayer of repentance - calling on God for mercy and forgiveness (Prov 28:13). There is something about mercy. A call for it attracts divine attention. Mercy can be described as a door that leads to God's treasury. In Mark 10:46-52, The man Bartmaeus (a blind man), had a desperate need. Rather than asked for restoration of his two eyes, he cried out for mercy. Jesus heard his voice and commanded that he be brought. Thereafter, Bartimaeus got his needed miracle. May your miracles reach you even as you ask for God's mercy in Jesus Name!

I don't know in what area you need help, my prayer is that God will send you the help you need, & may that help add value to your life and destiny. For this to happen and reach you on time, get rid of sin, abstain from all appearances of evil. Stay blessed.

CHAPTER 9

DIVINE VISITATION
(John 5:2-9)

The above Text is about a man who had the basic challenge of ill health. The Bible described him as someone *"having an infirmity of 38 years"*.

His health challenge brought other challenges. For instance, because he was not well, he could not work. Because he had no job, it means he had no income. Because he had no income, it means he was very poor & lonely. In addition, he had been at one point for sometime. This means that he was also stagnant & probably already abandoned to fate!

When a man is going through all these, it is likely he would feel frustrated. He may even attempt to kill himself!

In search for solution, he may have gone to several places - hospitals, churches, prophets, witch doctors, etc. Finally, someone may have told him: 'there is a Pool called "Bethesda", go there & you will be healed'. He went there (or he was carried there). However, his problem did not disappear overnight. Days passed, weeks came & gone.

Months rolled by & turned into years, yet nothing happened. BUT one day like today, JESUS paid him a visit. The man experienced A Divine Visitation, and his story changed for the better & forever! May the Lord pay you a special visittoday, & may your story change for the better in Jesus Name, Amen. There are some lessons to note.

First, every one - be it a man or woman, old, young, boy or girl, big or small, has a challenge. Some challenges are physical, some are spiritual. Some are financial while some are marital. Some challenges are career related, while some are academic, emotional, & so on.

For example, there was a man. He had been enjoying good health. He also had an early & smooth education even up to the highest Degree. He had no extra-ordinary challenge in life. Then he got married, & the years of waiting began. He waited nine solid years. Thank God, He visited them not too long ago, & he is now a father of more than one child!

A woman was always receiving 2 strange visitors at midnight. They would come into her bedroom through the wall. Their business was mainly to beat her up, & this they did mercilessly! After that, they would depart the same way they had come - through the walls! Thank God for His mercies. She was prayed for,& God ended her troubles.

Sometime ago, a man approached a Pastor & said "Pastor, I need prayers. Nearly all who promised or offered to help me always ended up in trouble!" It was very obvious that he needed help. We thank God He stepped into his case to set him free.

Second, God is a God of mercy. He is also a God of equal opportunity. Out of His mercy, here, He made some help available to all who were sick at the Pool. The Bible said: *'at a certain time, an Angel came down & stirred the water such that anyone* (no matter the nature of his/her problem), *who stepped into the pool after the stirring would be healed* (Vs 4). Thank God for His mercy. That you are still alive today is only by the mercy of God (see Lam 3:20-24; Rom 9:15-16). In not too distant past, I was in a city traffic & some Blind Beggars ran up to our car asking us for alms. The Driver, - a fellow Christian, shouted on them. Almost immediately, I heard the Lord speak quietly to me: "They (the Beggars) could have been in this car while you could have been the one outside - blind & begging"! This prompted me to gently rebuke & caution our Brother - Driver. Thank God for His mercies. That you are who & where you are is by the mercy of God!

Here, God also gave each person an equal opportunity to get his or her miracle (John 3:16-18; Titus 3:3-4). We thank God that even today, salvation is still freely available today to ALL!:

> *"9 That if thou shalt confess with thy mouth the Lord Jesus, and shalt believe in thine heart that God hath raised him from the dead, thou shalt be saved. 10 For with the heart a man believeth unto righteousness; and with the mouth confession is made unto salvation. 11 For the scripture saith, Whosoever believeth on him shall not be ashamed. 12 For there is no difference between the Jew and the Greek: for the same Lord over all is rich unto all that call upon him. 13 For whosoever shall call upon the name of the Lord shall be saved."*

Third, even though help was very near, this man could not access it! The help did not reach him. According to him, two things prevented him: he had no one to put him in the water after the stirring by an Angel. Also, even when he made personal efforts to get there, someone always got there before him. In other words, someone, somehow always hijacked or snatched his miracle!! As you read this, may be you are like this man, someone is always there snatching or hijacking your miracle, your blessing, your promotion, & the help meant for you. I pray for you right away, may every hijacker of your blessing - whether man woman, demons, or even Satan himself - be arrested NOW in Jesus Name. Amen!

Fourth, one day, Jesus came for the man - just for him alone. He is where you are right now - just for you & you only. May you not miss your miracle.

The Bible went on in Verse 6: *"Jesus saw the man & knew he had been in that condition for a long time"*. This tells us something very important about Jesus: When He sees a man or woman, He knows everything about him or her, I mean "EVERYTHING" - his or her past, present & future.

This is because He - Jesus is all-seeing. He is also the Alpha & Omega. In addition, He made all men (see Rev 4:11; Rev 1:18). Jesus sees & knows what a man is running after & what is running after the man. He knows what a man is pursuing & what is pursuing the man. He knows the problems, the aches, & the fears of every man. Perhaps you also need to realize that Jesus even sees & knows the schemes, devices & the motives in the heart of every human being (Luke 19:1-10; John 4:28-29).

There is a Good News however: Not only does Jesus sees & knows everything about every man, He also has the power to meet every need. May God meet you right now at you very point of need in Jesus Name.

Fifth, till in Verse 6 (of our Bible Text), Jesus asked this man what one would ordinarily call an unnecessary question: *"Do you want to be made whole?"*. The truth is that not all who have problems want a godly solution. Some who appear to want it may not want it as urgently as you think!

The General Overseer of our Church (we affectionately call him "Daddy G.O"), told us the story of a woman he went topray for who requested that he (Daddy G.O) should pray that her sickness should go away gradually! There was a similar case like that in the Bible:

9 And Moses said unto Pharaoh, Glory over me: when shall I intreat for thee, and for thy servants, and for thy people, to destroy the frogs from thee and thy houses, that they may remain in the river only? 10 And he said, To morrow. And he said, Be it according to thy word: that thou mayest know that there is none like unto the LORD our God." (Exod 8:9-10).

I vividly remember the story of a Blind young man who came to my office begging for money to buy the Braille. The Holy Spirit impressed it very strongly upon my heart that we should pray for him because God was willing & prepared to heal him. I went to the young man & told him that God wanted to restore his eyes. He refused blatantly! He said he did not want any prayers. He said further that all he needed was money to buy his Braille!

I don't know what you are going through right now. If God were to ask you now: *"DO YOU WANT A MIRACLE?"* What will be your answer - 'Yes' or 'No'? If God asks you further,*"When do you want the miracle?"* What would you say?

May be you are yet to be sure of your relationship with God, You can right now. Acts 4:12 says:

"Neither is there Salvation in any other, for there is no other Name given under Heaven, among men whereby we must be saved!"

This tells us 2 very important things: Salvation is a MUST (II Cor 5:10-11; Rom 6:23). Also, that ONLY Jesus can make it available (John 15:13). You will be saved only when we have acknowledged & confessed your sins (I John 1:5-9; Prov 28:13; Rev 3:20). The time to be saved is NOW! It is in your interest to be saved (II Cor 6:2; Rom 8:31; Gen 39:2-3). It's time to pray:

- Father, thank You for Your word (John 8:32).
- Father, increase my faith in You.
- Father, turn every challenge I am facing to testimonies.
- Father, I command in the Name of Jesus that every force - both human & spiritual, that has been positioned to hijack my miracle be relocated. If they don't want to relocate gently, Father dislocate them!
- Father, where there had been no man to help me, please help me today. Please help me right now!
- Father, please visit me right now & change my story for good.

** (Be free to add any other requests you may have).

God will hear & surprise you in Jesus Name, Amen!

CHAPTER 10

DIVINE ENCOUNTER
(Luke 17:11-19)

The story in the above Text, is a classical case of a DIVINE ENCOUNTER. When He was here physically, our Lord Jesus made several trips between Capernaum - His ministry base in Galilee (Northern part of Israel), & Jerusalem in Judea (Southern Israel). Located in-between Galilee & Judea is the land of Samaria. On different occasions, Jesus went through different routes. For example, in John 4, He had to pass through a Town called Sychar, because the whole Town needed to hear the Gospel. The woman by the Well became the link to them. In John 4:39-47, the Bible said the whole city came to believe Jesus. He, Jesus, eventually spent 2-3 more days with them.

On this particular occasion (Luke 17), our Lord Jesus chose to go through a certain Village (not named). Why did He have to? It is because some men (about 10 of them) had a need that MUST BE MET - a need that could not wait any longer. A need that must not be carried over to a new week, a new month, or a New Year. This book is not in your hand right now just by accident. It may be because you need an urgent intervention. It may be because the enemy has beenmocking you - asking where is your God! That was exactly the case with Hannah. You may have been writing an examination several times without passing. You may have been applying for work with no success. You may even be sick right now. Today, God will surprise you for good in Jesus Name, Amen!

Let us take some lessons from this very important passage of Scriptures (Luke 17:11-19):

A closer look at the ten men mentioned here, tells us a lot. They had a peculiar problem - they were lepers - they were outcasts, a social menace. In those days in the land of Israel, it was believed that leprosy was contagious. So, no one was allowed to come near or touch them. It was also seen as a curse. It was believed that it is only those whom God was angry with who became leprous. For example, Miriam (Numbers 12:1-15). The same with, Gehazi (II Kings 5:19-27, & King Uzziah (II Chronicles 26:16-23).

You may not be physically leprous, but your case may appear so. Situations may have been making you to hide from people. You may be in a huge debt - owing a lot of money! Also, people may be avoiding you like a plague because your ways are just unusual. You may be like the man called Nabal (I Sam 25:17) - no one can talk to you or correct you. Of course, you may have become so ill or sick that those close to you have abandoned you to fate! Today, in the Might Name of Jesus, you will experience a Divine Encounter, & God will send you the help you need in Jesus Name.

These Lepers did not look or search for Jesus. Rather, it was Jesus who, by a special divine arrangement, went their way. Today, God will reach you right where you are, & meet you at the very point where the shoe is pinching you, inJesus Name. He will step into your health, your marriage, your home, your office, your academics, & your spiritual life. Are you in a situation in which your marriage is about to be broken? Is the divorce paper already served you? God will intervene in Jesus Name. The enemy that has intruded into your home shall go back to sender in Jesus Name. Perhaps your concern is the fear of being deported or sent back home. You may even voluntarily going back home because you have virtually nothing to show for the several years you've been away. FEAR NOT! - You will not return empty- handed. God will terminate every failure in your life.

The Lepers (in our Text), used what they had to get what they needed: Though leprous, they could still see, they could hear, talk, & even walk (though slowly). Thank God, they lifted up their voices to Jesus & attracted His attention. Many times, we focus on what we lack & never realize how blessed & rich we are already. This has happened to me several times before:

Some years ago, while serving as a State Pastor in our Church (somewhere in South-Western part of Nigeria), two women came in for prayers. The younger was in an advanced stage of pregnancy. She said that the current pregnancy was the seventh, but she had only one child alive! We prayed with her, & counseled her to travel to the Redemption Camp (of the TRCCG, on Lagos/Ibadan Expressway), for more prayers & especially for spiritual covering against all satanic assault over her baby on the way. To the glory of God, she obeyed, & her baby lived!

However, after the two women left my office that day, I locked the door & laid prostrate on the floor. I repented of my heart of ingratitude for several blessings & in particular those of marital fruitfulness, conception, safe carrying, & easy deliveries I have been enjoying. I also took time tothank God for healthy, great & wonderful children which the Lord had been gracious enough to give to us (Gen 32:10; Gen 33:5; Isa 8:18).

I once also had an encounter in which the Lord challenged my heart which had been blinded by needs rather than gratitude. It happened in Ikeja (Lagos, South-West of Nigeria). I just got down from a public transport. As I was walking down the street, suddenly the Lord focused my

Divine Encounter

attention on a man going a few meters ahead of me - he was limping. The message became clear: I was walking straight & easily! There & then, I repented & began praising God for my two legs. You too may have been like me. May God deliver us from a heart of ingratitude. The man King David warned in Psalm 103:1-5:

"1 Bless the LORD, O my soul: and all that is within me, bless his holy name. 2 Bless the LORD, O my soul, and forget not all his benefits: 3 Who forgiveth all thine iniquities; who healeth all thy diseases; 4 Who redeemeth thy life from destruction; who crowneth thee with lovingkindness and tender mercies; 5 Who satisfieth thy mouth with good things; so that thy youth is renewed like the eagle's."

In Vs 13 of our Text, one can observe the wisdom of the ten Lepers- they asked for something very special. Thy asked Jesus for **"MERCY"** - not miracles, of food, money, healing, & so on. Many people don't know the importance of what is called 'MERCY', & why they needed it.

Among other things, *'mercy'* has been defined as *"a blessing that is an act of divine favor or compassion"* Mercy is that thing that moves God to give us what we least deserve. For instance, our sins qualify us for death & eternal punishment (Rom 3:23; Rom 6:23; II Cor 5:21).

"11 For as the heaven is high above the earth, so great is his

mercy toward them that fear him....17 But the mercy of the LORD is from everlasting to everlasting upon them that fear him, and his righteousness unto children's children;....22 It is of the LORD'S mercies that we are not consumed, because his compassions fail not. 23 They are new every morning: great is thy faithfulness...15 For he saith to Moses, I will have mercy on whom I will have mercy, and I will have compassion on whom I will have compassion. 16 So then it is not of him that willeth, nor of him that runneth, but of God that sheweth mercy....13 He that covereth his sins shall not prosper: but whoso confesseth and forsaketh them shall have mercy." (Psalm 103:11,17; Lam 3: 22-24; Rom 9:15-16; Prov 28:13).

God is very rich & very great in mercy. We can never ask for too much of God's mercy.

The man, David always received help from God. The reason may be because he always appealed to God for MERCY! - a look at many of his prayers, will show you what I mean.

For the man - Blind Bartimaeus, it was his cry for mercy that attracted Jesus to him. At the end of the day he got his long awaited miracle (see Mark 10:46-52).

Our God is Sovereign! This means He has the final say (Lam 3:37). He also has His perfect times for whatever He does. God's timing is always right & perfect. When God's time arrives, NOTHING can hinder or stand in His way (Psalm 102:13). May today be your day in Jesus Name.

The story of Joseph is a good illustration of this very fact. He was imprisoned for an offense which he never committed. He poured out his heart to a man who could help him out of prison. However, for two solid years, the man forgot Joseph! Thank God He didn't forget Joseph. When Joseph's time in God's agenda came, all that God needed to do was to give Pharaoh 2 strange dreams which troubled him, & which none of his magicians could decode. Pharaoh must therefore look for Joseph! At the end of the day, Joseph was elevated to the position of a Prime aminister - even in a foreign land. In a no distant future, may you too be sought for - in your office, in your community in Jesus Name. May the Lord make you the solution to their problems & needs.

God's Sovereignty also means He controls time. He can reverse, rewind, & fast-forward time as well as events. It was because the day for the 10 Lepers had come, that Jesus had to pass through their location. As the Lord passes through your City today, may He not pass you bye in Jesus Name.

Still talking about the Sovereignty of God, it will be noted that the miracle the Lepers needed happened as the men went into the city in obedience to the instruction of Jesus. It could have taken place instantly as in the cases of Naman, in II Kings 5: 13-15:

"13 And his servants came near, and spake unto him, and said, My father, if the prophet had bid thee do some great thing, wouldest thou not have done it? how much rather then, when he saith to thee, Wash, and be clean? 14 Then went he down, and dipped himself seven times in Jordan, according to the saying of the man of God: and his flesh came again like unto the flesh of a little child, and he was clean. 15 And he returned to the man of God, he and all his company, and came, and stood before him: and he said, Behold, now I know that there is no God in all earth, but in Israel: now therefore, I pray thee, take a blessing of thy servant." (see also Matt 8:1-3).In all ways possible - whether where you are right now, or on your way home, or as you reach home today, - may the Lord God surprise you in Jesus Name.

Finally, one can see faith & obedience at work here:

"17 So then faith cometh by hearing, and hearing by the word of God...20 He sent his word, and healed them, and delivered them from their destructions." (Rom 10:17; Psalm 107: 20).

The word they heard, believed, & obeyed here is "GO YE & SHOW YOURSELVES TO THE PRIESTS". I don't know what God had been saying to you since you started

Divine Encounter

reading this book. DON'T TAKE IT FOR GRANTED! Don't see it as a man's word or a voice from the Devil. ACT ON IT! (See Rom 8:14; Isaiah 55: 9-11). I pray that God's word will prosper in your life & situation in Jesus Name. The Word shall heal you, deliver you, make way for you, & restore you. It will uproot & dismantle every obstacle or obstruction in your way in Jesus Name.

Perhaps you yet to have a personal relationship with Jesus (see Psalm 107: 17-19; I John 1:5-9; Rom 6:1-2; Prov 28:13).

You may join in praying as follows:

1. Father, thank you for Your Word (John 8:32). Thank You for speaking to me. I believe Your Word, please let Your Word work for me - let it work in my body, in my soul, in my spirit.

Your city & Nation need your prayers. Why don't you take some moment & intercede. Ask God to have mercy & protect all who are doing what is right in His eyes. Ask God to also convict evil doers & bring them to repentance. And, if they would not, He should bring them to a speedy judgment!

CHAPTER 11

COMMITMENT
(Hebrew 1:9)

A closer look at our Text shows that there are some things God loves, and there are things that He hates. Of course, there are some things which God does not only hate, they are abominations to Him (see Ps 15:1-5; Prov 6:16-19; Luke 16:15; Matt 15:1-3, 6-9).

It takes Commitment to love or hate what another person loves or hates. In Amos 3:3, we read:

"Can two walk together, except they be agreed?"

Another version/translation puts it this way:

"Is it possible for two to go walking together, if not by agreement?" (Basic English). See also John 14:15; Prov 8:13.

What then is 'Commitment'? It is a promise or an agreement to do something in the future for, or, with somebody. It is also to be bound emotionally & intellectually to a course of action (or to another person).

Marks or evidences of commitment include: allegiance,

101

dedication, loyalty, trust, etc.

It has been noted that some things enhance or promote Commitment. These include, knowledge, availability, faithfulness, sacrifice, patience, endurance, & gratitude orappreciation. Here, we shall focus two of them, viz, 'knowledge', and 'availability'.

To 'know' or have 'knowledge' of something means to some good extent, you are not totally ignorant of that thing.

Knowledge can general or partial. It can also be specific or specialized. It can be about the past, the present, or even the future. For instance, it is when we read Romans

4:17-21, that we come to understand & appreciate the basis for the great faith in God which the man Abraham demonstrated in Gen 22:1-18. Rom 4: 17-21 declares:

"17 (As it is written, I have made thee a father of many nations,) before him whom he believed, even God, who quickeneth the dead, and calleth those things which be not as though they were. 18 Who against hope believed in hope, that he might become the father of many nations; according to that which was spoken, So shall thy seed be. 19 And being not weak in faith, he considered not his own body now dead, when he was about an hundred years old, neither yet the deadness of Sarah's womb: 20 He staggered

not at the promise of God through unbelief; but was strong in faith, giving glory to God; 21 And being fully persuaded that, what he had promised, he was able also to perform." (See Daniel 11:32b, Phil 3:7-10; Rom 8: 35-39).

Here, based on the knowledge that the man Abraham had about God, - HE IS ABLE TO DO WHAT HE HAD

PROMISED, he, Abraham refused to yield to all limiting evidences in & around him. The Amplified Version of the Bible put Verse 18 of the above passage this way:

"For Abraham, human reasons (for) hope being gone, hoped in faith that he should become the father of nations, as he had been promised, so (numberless) shall your descendants be".

When all human reasons for hope are gone, may God help you & I to still hope & have in Him!

If knowledge enhances commitment, it follows that ignorance will certainly limit or hinder commitment!

It is important to point out that not all which knowledge brings, or we come to know will be pleasant & easy to swallow! John 6: 53-68 brings us to a typical day in the earthly ministry of our Lord Jesus Christ. Let us look at the passage together:

"53 Then Jesus said unto them, Verily, verily, I say unto you, Except ye eat the flesh of the Son of man, and drink his blood, ye have no life in you. 54 Whoso eateth my flesh, and drinketh my blood, hath eternal life; and I will raise him up at the last day. 55 For my flesh is meat indeed, and my blood is drink indeed. 56 He that eateth my flesh, and drinketh my blood, dwelleth in me, and I in him. 57 As the living Father hath sent me, and I live by the Father: so he that eateth me, even he shall live by me. 58 This is that bread which came down from heaven: not as your fathers did eat manna, and are dead: he that eateth of this bread shall live for ever. 59 These things said he in the synagogue, as he taught in Capernaum. 60 Many therefore of his disciples, when they had heard this, said, This is an hard saying; who can hear it? 61 When Jesus knew in himself that his disciples murmured at it, he said unto them, Doth this offend you? 62 What and if ye shall see the Son of man ascend up where he was before? 63 It is the spirit that quickeneth; the flesh profiteth nothing: the words that I speak unto you, they are spirit, and they are life. 64 But there are some of you that believe not. For Jesus knew from the beginning who they were that believed not, and who should betray him. 65 And he said, Thereforesaid I unto you, that no man can come unto me, except it were given unto him of my Father. 66 From that time many of his disciples went back, and walked no more with him. 67 Then said Jesus unto the twelve, Will ye also go away? 68

Then Simon Peter answered him, Lord, to whom shall we go? thou hast the words of eternal life."

Our Lord had several followers. All along He had been exposing them to basic issues of Discipleship. On this very day He went a little deeper, & said any one who did not eat His flesh & also drink His blood had no life! Several of the Disciples looked at each other & said 'what is He talking about, we did not bargain for this'! One by one they went away. Eventually the Lord turned to the inner Twelve & asked them: 'Won't you too go away?' Peter responded: 'To whom shall we go? You alone has the Word of life'. In other words, Peter was saying: "we are already in it together, no matter 'the thick or the thin', we are not backing out"! That is true commitment.

To be available means you are there, where & when it matters. God wants us to be available, & to make available to Him, all that we are, all that we have, all that we will be, & all that we will ever have. He deserves to have them & have the best of them all - our life, our health, wealth, our intellect, our competences, our gifts, talents, & our money, etc.

Talking about or time, we are to give God the best of each day. We are to begin our days in His presence - with gratitude (see Psalm 100:1-5; Lam 3:22-26).

Someone jokingly said if the first voice you hear when you wake up in the morning is "post office", "post office", that can not be from God but from the enemy who is all out to distract you, rob you of God's presence, & thereby disorganized your day, & life in general. What a truth! Today, many of us don't run to the physical post office. The post office is right in our bedroom. The first place many visit when they wake up is their e-mail box, the face book, the U- Tube, or Whatsap, etc! They check mails, & from there other distractions & diversions follow. By the time they realize it, the early & very vital hours they should have spent with God is wasted or stolen from them by the enemy Satan (John 10:10).

Let us look at some examples in Commitment:

The first is God Himself. In John 3:16-18, we read:

"16 For God so loved the world, that he gave his only begotten Son, that whosoever believeth in him should not perish, but have everlasting life. 17 For God sent not his Son into the world to condemn the world; but that the world through him might be saved. 18 He that believeth on him is not condemned: but he that believeth not is condemned already, because he hath not believed in the name of the only begotten Son of God."

This means that God Himself was so much committed to the project of salvaging mankind that He gave His best &

only begotten Son to it. The same with our Lord Jesus Christ. In John 15:13 & Heb 12: 1-3, the Bible records:

"13 Greater love hath no man than this, that a man lay down his life for his friends....1 Wherefore seeing we also are compassed about with so great a cloud of witnesses, let us lay aside every weight, and the sin which doth so easily beset us, and let us run with patience the race that is set before us, 2 Looking unto Jesus the author and finisher of our faith; who for the joy that was set before him endured the cross, despising the shame, and is set down at the right hand of the throne of God. 3 For consider him that endured such contradiction of sinners against himself, lest ye be wearied and faint in your minds."

We had earlier looked at the man Abraham. The blessings of his commitment were generational. It flowed to his children, & children's children. Today, it is still flowing even to the whole world (see Gen 22: 1-18; Rom 4: 17-21).

What of Paul the Apostle? Acts 21:11-14 says this about him:

"11 And when he was come unto us, he took Paul's girdle, and bound his own hands and feet, and said, Thus saith the Holy Ghost, So shall the Jews at Jerusalem bind the man that owneth this girdle, and shall deliver him into the hands of the Gentiles. 12 And when we heard these things, both we, and they of that place, besought him not to go up

to Jerusalem. 13 Then Paul answered, What mean ye to weep and to break mine heart? for I am ready not to be bound only, but also to die at Jerusalem for the name of the Lord Jesus. 14 And when he would not be persuaded, we ceased, saying, The will of the Lord be done."

The final example we want to look at is that of the man in Mark 9: 17-27. He was the father of a boy with several challenges. His son was being tormented by demons. He did not abandon or disown the boy (in spite of all the heartaches & embarrassment he went through). In appealing to Jesus to intervene, this committed father said: "this MY son..."

Let me conclude this chapter with the words of insight from Apostle Paul in Rom 8: 28; 35-39:

"28 And we know that all things work together for good to them that love God, to them who are the called according to his purpose....35 Who shall separate us from the love of Christ? shall tribulation, or distress, or persecution, or famine, or nakedness, or peril, or sword? 36 As it is written, For thy sake we are killed all the day long; we are accounted as sheep for the slaughter. 37 Nay, in all these things we are more than conquerors through him that loved us. 38 For I am persuaded, that neither death, nor life, nor angels, nor principalities, nor powers, nor things present, nor things to come, 39 Nor height, nor depth, nor

any other creature, shall be able to separate us from the love of God, which is in Christ Jesus our Lord."

May the Lord help you to love what God loves, & to hate what He hates. May He also help you to increase your commitment to Him & His Kingdom in Jesus Name, Amen.

CHAPTER 12

VICTORY AT THE GATES!

The desire of every human is to be a success in all we attempt or lay our hands upon in life. To be defeated is seen as an anomaly. Victory is sweet & desirable. It is a sign that someone has gone to battle, fought gallantly, & returned with laurels. Have you suffered some defeat in life? God is bringing you into a new season - a season & era of victory.

For every victory, there are keys or strategies.

What is a Gate?

It is a means of entrance or exit. A door, valve or other device for controlling the passage of things (especially of fluids). It is also a point/place of meeting by Elders - where critical transactions/decisions are made. Gates are intended for Many reasons - they may be to secure/protect what is kept inside, prevent intruders, etc.

In some cases, gate are installed at entry points to nations, cities/towns, lives.

Gates can also refer to strongholds that are installed to compete/hinder progress/fruitfulness, etc.

Gates can be physical or spiritual. Some men are gates. They can allow or hinder those they lead or represent from being free, or made to remain in bondage. Several Gates are mentioned in the Bible. For example, the gates of Jericho; the Gates of Jerusalem; the gates of Heaven/Kingdom; the Gates of Hell; the Gates to Nations or Cities; etc.

There are other forms of gates that were not directly mentioned in the Scriptures, but are equally real. For instance, Calendar gates - they mark the beginning of a New year, a New month, a New week, a New day, etc. Often in the past, I have had to ask my self the critical question of when a day actually start or begin! The beginning or start of a project or a programme can also be referred to as it's gate, & what happens there can have a serious bearing on the success or otherwise of the project.

Also, there are Gates to the human life - these are the organs or senses through which we do receive &, absorb or release various things that positively (& negatively) affect our lives, our health, our attitude, & ultimately our destiny.

These gates include our eyes, our ears, our mouth, mind, hands, feet, etc (see Col 3:1-5; Rom 6:12-13, 16-19). Several times in the Bible, we are counselled or commanded to be careful of what we see or watch, hear, touch or handle, as well as what we say or eat, where we go & what we do there. We are also warned to keep our mind and heart pure because what we think upon can determine who we become. Victory and/or defeat are all determined at the gates.

Virtually, all gates have keys that can lock or open them. Life in general requires some definite actions at the Gates. If such actions are not timely taken or we fail to take such actions, it may lead to calamities and lasting regrets.

ALL gates are meant to be possessed. By this we mean that we are to be in control - determining events at such gates (& not vice versa). A man who is a victim at the gatewhere he ought to be a victor, has already lost the battle or chance of success (see Isa 40:3-5; Exod 20:6; Isa 1:19; Isa 3:10; Psalm1:1-3). Part of the actions to take at some gates may be to dismantle, pull down, uproot or use a superior key to unlock or open them. (Jer 1:9-10; II Cor 10:3-5; Ephes 6:10-18).

Now, let's take closer look at some specific Gates: The Gates of Jericho:

In Joshua 6: 1-6, we are told that the gates to this Great City was shut, & that nothing & no one could enter in or go out.

The city of Jericho was very strategic to Joshua as a leader of God's people. Two things happened before the hosts of Israel got there physically. First, God had spoken assuring them that HE had given them the City. Also as part of his military strategy, Joshua had sent an advanced Team to survey the terrain. It was that team that Rahab hosted & testified to that 'the whole city had heard about all that the God of Israel did for HIS people'. And moreover fear had gripped all in the City. For saving the spies, the woman was to be spared with all her family. So when the Israelites arrived at the Gates of Jericho & found it shut & barred, they were not moved. The gates had already been possessed spiritually. The result is now history. God gave a resounding victory over every resistance. At the end, Joshua commanded that the city be razed to the ground. He also pronounced a curse on any one who would ever attempt to rebuild the city. There are many people, particularly God's children after receiving clear & sure word from the Lord detailing what they needed to do to have their victory, they look at physical circumstances, go for 'expert' advice, etc, rather than act upon the word of God. Our God has advanced information on all events, all men, & is always far ahead of the enemy. In II Chronicles 20, three Nations formed an ally to attack the land of Judah. Like any King, Jehoshaphat was initially afraid & troubled. But his fear drove him to God's presence where he eventually got the key to posses the gates of the battle.

Among other things, God assured him that the battle was not Jehoshaphat's but God's. One of the things that struck me in the episode was what God said through His prophet to the king & his people. In verses 15-18, God told King Jehoshaphat where to pitch its tent. There were two basic reasons behind this. First, God knew the route the enemies were taking. Second, God knew quite well how far the enemies would have gone & that they would never have been able to go beyond that point by the following day! I don't know which battles you are presently fighting or the route or strategy the enemy have adopted to fight you. I may not also know who their allies are. One thing is very sure: God knows it all. He also has power to arrest, paralyze & confound them. King Jehoshaphat possessed the gates of his enemies when he ran to the house of the Lord to seek HIS face, & by also declaring a national fasting & prayer. It was the key that God gave him that he used to obtain all round victory!

The Gates of Jerusalem

The City of Jerusalem is both physically & spiritually significant to God & His Kingdom agenda especially His time table for the entire universe. It is the city God chose to put His Name & where He promised King David & all his descendants that HE would defend & protect from intruders provided the Israelites kept obeying Him. At the dedication of the Temple built by King Solomon, God committed Himself to making the City of Jerusalem special & unique.

Not less than twelve Gates entered the City. In effect thesetwelve Gates also open unto the whole world! They have become points of contact to pray for the whole world, and today, 24/7 prayers are mobilized both ways - for & from Jerusalem.

The gates of Heaven & of the Kingdom

When physically here on the Earth, our Lord Jesus spoke of 'the Kingdom of Heaven' or 'the kingdom of God' (as differently & respectively used in the Gospels of Matthew & Luke). In Matthew 25, HE used the parables of the 10 Virgins & that of the Talents to illustrate the importance of watching to the end, as well as the critical need to faithfully maximize our God-given endowments for God's glory.

The Gates of Hell

In Matt 6:16-18, our Lord Jesus, through an opinion poll, wanted to know if His closer followers really knew who He was. Peter eventually spoke: "You are Christ, the Son of the Living God"! Jesus then made a very fundamental statement: " .... And upon this rock I will built my Church, & the gates of hell will not prevail against it".

There is Hell - the ultimate end of all that do wickedly. There are also some semblances - forces, powers, authorities, places, & situations that represent hell in our world. They have a common identity & agenda: to hinder, work against, or out rightly stop the establishment of God's Kingdom on earth. Their target of attack is the Church which is the main vehicle God has purposed to use (Ephes 3:15). They also target the Family as an institution that must be destroyed or redefined &/or destabilized to achieve their evil agenda.

Thank God that when He wants to get something done, NO power in heaven, on the earth or underneath the earth can stop Him. That is why all the enemies of the Church hadbeen doing over the age had not succeeded & will never succeed in wiping out the Church! Of course, when we talk about the Church we are not referring to the buildings or places of worship. We are simply talking about the church corporate as well as you -the individual Believer. Whatever you may be going through as challenges - whether, physical, marital, academic, career-wise, the Lord will give you victory. The Gates of Hell will not prevail against you. All things will work together for your good. You will laugh last.

Gates to Nations & Cities

Every nation & city has gates to it. These gates are both physical & spiritual. Some of them are institutional, with critical personalities behind them. For example,

Parliaments & Parliamentarians, Air & Seaports, Corporate & Government institutional apparatuses. Through these gates policies, decisions, & people & goods enter & pass to the land & populace.

Technological Gate

In our 'modern' high-tech world, this gate has probably become the most important gate that has the highest potential influence & effect on human existence - both for good & for evil. Everywhere one goes - at home, on the road, in the air, during the day as well as at night, in remote & urban areas, our World seem to have been invaded by the 'power of the air'!

Calendar Gates

Each new day, week, month & year has its gates. The Enemy can always grab it, divert, hijack & help you misuse or out rightly waste it. That is why you must start each day, week, month & Year with gratitude to God, & in prayer & His Word, so it can be a useful & fruitful one.

The Gates to the human life

These refer to the organs/senses (- the eyes, ears, mouth, mind, hands, feet, etc). What has been happening at the gates to your life. Has the enemy taken over? May be you have become a victim at the critical gates of your life, & you hardly can control or restrain what you see, hear, think about, what you touch or take. May be you cannot control or restrain where you go or who you follow. Jesus can help you. He can liberate you & keep you free (John 8:32, 36).

In Col 3:1-5; Rom 6:12-13, 16-19, the Bible says:

"1 If ye then be risen with Christ, seek those things which are above, where Christ sitteth on the right hand of God. 2 Set your affection on things above, not on things on the earth. 3 For ye are dead, and your life is hid with Christ in God. 4 When Christ, who is our life, shall appear, then shall ye also appear with him in glory. 5 Mortify therefore your members which are upon the earth; fornication, uncleanness, inordinate affection, evil concupiscence, and covetousness, which is idolatry:....12 Let not sin therefore reign in your mortal body, that ye should obey it in the lusts thereof. 13 Neither yield ye your members as instruments of unrighteousness unto sin: but yield yourselves unto God, as those that are alive from the dead, and your members as instruments of righteousness unto God...16 Know ye not, that to whom ye yield yourselves servants to obey, his servants ye are to whom ye obey; whether of sin unto death, or of obedience unto righteousness? 17 But God be thanked, that ye were the servants of sin, but ye have obeyed from the heart that form of doctrine which was delivered you. 18 Being then made free from sin, ye became the servants of righteousness. 19 I speak after the manner of men because

of the infirmity of your flesh: for as ye have yielded your members servants to uncleanness and to iniquity unto iniquity; even so now yield your members servants to righteousness unto holiness."

Also, there is need for you to learn to stand in the gap for children & their future. This in fact should be very important to you. As God has specific agenda & programmes as well as personalities He plans to use to accomplish them in each generation, so also the Devil targets each generation to try to prevent such godly plans from seeing the light of the day. May your place& those of your children in God's programme for your generation & theirs, never be thwarted in Jesus Name. The man Job was very much aware of this fact.

Hence he daily took his sons & daughters to God everyday in prayer. He was an interceding father (see Job 1:1-5; Psalm 1:1-3).

Gate keepers

Gate Keepers are very influential & powerful. They are important to life. They can let you in or out, & vice versa! They can make & unmake you. This means Gate keepers can be a stumbling block to the freedom & liberty or even the destiny of those behind gates. In other words, Gate keepers are critical to life - both physically & spiritually. In some sense also, they can be pace setters. They drive the society. In certain cases they have succeeded in driving their generation in the wrong directions! In this instance, policy makers & researchers in industries like the Automobiles, textiles, food medicine, pharmaceuticals, & entertainment, etc are of great influence.Of more importance & influence are spiritual gate keepers. They can determine a man's destiny - whether a man makes Heaven or whether he ends up in Hell! The Lord Jesus accused the Scribes & Pharisees that they held the keys of life, & that not only were they not entering into God's Kingdom, they were also preventing those who wanted to enter (see Luke 11:37-52). Perhaps you are like the Scribes & Pharisees - you are standing in the way of sinners, blocking their entry into God's Kingdom by your wrong lifestyle even though you claim to be CHRISTIAN or a Minister of God. You are far from being an example of a true believer (I Cor 4:2; Rom 2:20-24). I call upon you to repent before it is too late for you. If you refuse & continue in your evil, be sure of one thing: God who is jealous of His Holy Name will intervene (Ezek 36: 20-23).

Victory at the Gates

The plan of God is that all His children & Servants experience victory at all the Gates. He has also put everything needed in place to ensure victory for His Church & Kingdom. Hence He told us what to do & how we should handle Gates. As mentioned earlier in this

Chapter, Gates are meant to be possessed, controlled, opened, shut, locked, dismantled and or uprooted (bar & locks), as the need arises. In Gen 22:18, God blessed & promised Abraham that his children will possess the gates of their enemies. In Psalm 127:5, God said our children will speak/ reply & handle the enemies at the gates. In Matt 16: 18-19, our Lord Jesus empowered His Church when He said: "Upon this rock I will build My Church, & the gates of hell will not prevail against it".

To show the very importance of victory at the gates to our human life, our Lord Jesus twice in the book of Matthew (5:27-30, 18: 8-9), said "If your right eye (& left too) causes you to sin, pluck it out... If your right hand (& left too) or foot makes you to sin, cut it off!

JESUS - the Lord & Controller of Gates

Gates can be controlled. What happens there can be handled by our Lord Jesus. He is the controller of Gates. In Lam 3:37 & Rev 3:7-8, the Bible declared the Sovereignty of God, & the power in the Name of Jesus:

"37 Who is he that saith, and it cometh to pass, when the Lord commandeth it not?...7 And to the angel of the church in Philadelphia write; These things saith he that is holy, he that is true, he that hath the key of David, he that openeth, and no man shutteth; and shutteth, and no man openeth; 8 I know thy works: behold, I have set before thee

an open door, and no man can shut it: for thou hast a little strength, and hast kept my word, and hast not denied my name."

The Holy Spirit:

The Holy Spirit too plays a very vital & important role in giving us victory at the Gates. He is powerful. More powerful than Gate Keepers! He, the Holy Spirit, can open & close Gates. For example, He can open prison gates & set the captives free. He can also dismantle & uproot gates (including their bars & locks)! When the Holy Spirit was upon Samson, He caused him to uproot the gate that was meant to hold him captive. Not only this, the Holy Spirit can compel, enable or restrain Gate Keepers. What has been happening at the Gates of your life, your office, your city, & Nation? Why don't you hand them over to the Holy Spirit. He will step in & give you beautiful testimonies.

OPEN HEAVENS

(Matters Arising)

This is a special section of this book. The materials here arose as a result of personal meditation on several subjects covered. May the Holy Spirit provoke in you question & issues that will help your Christian life & destiny in Jesus Name.

Joshua & Destiny

(Joshua 1:3-4; 13:1)

"Every place that the sole of your foot shall tread upon, to you have I given it, as I spake unto Moses. From the wilderness, and this Lebanon, even unto the great river, the river Euphrates, all the land of the Hittites, and unto the great sea toward the going down of the sun, shall be your border.... Now Joshua was old and well stricken in years; and Jehovah said unto him, Thou art old and well stricken in years, and there remaineth yet very much land to be possessed." (Joshua 1:3-4, 13:1)

Here, God spelt out in clear terms what Joshua, the successor to Moses (that great man of God) was called to do. God went to the extent of giving him even the geographical boundaries of the land to be possessed. More importantly however, are four particular promises of God to Joshua:

(a) Every place that the soul of your foot will tread upon I have given you (Vs 3),

(b) No man shall be able to stand before you all the days of your life (Vs 5),

(c) As I was with Moses, so I will be with you (Vs 5),

(d) I will not leave you nor forsake you (Vs 5),

Years rolled by, several efforts & conquests were made. Then God showed up again & said something very strange in chapter 13:1 - *"Thou art old & well stricken in years, & there remaineth yet very much land to be possessed"* (not just to be entered but to be possessed!).

Matters Arising:

- What happened over the years that even in his old age 'there (still) remained yet very much land to be possessed"?

- Did God under estimate the assignment or the capability of Joshua, or both?

- Was there so much diversion/distraction/dissipation of energy on wrong things - eg, settling of quarrels & disputes, etc that he had little time left for the essentials? Did the urgent prevent him from the important? (See Acts 6:3-4).

- Were there so many 'dead woods' in Joshua's team which he refused to get rid of? People one could refer to as "Executive liabilities"?

- Did little successes limit him from bigger achievements?

- Did Joshua have some personal, &/or marital challenges that became hindrances to fulfilling destiny?

Are you a leader of some sort? Are you a leader of a large organization? Are you concerned that you are growing old & succession has become a major issue?

As you weigh your life, & leadership by all these, may the Holy Spirit enlighten & give you strategies that will help you finish well finish strong - without scars in Jesus Name.

Special Thanksgiving (Better than Mama Naomi):

(Ruth 1:3-5, 19-21)

"3 And Elimelech Naomi's husband died; and she was left, and her two sons. 4 And they took them wives of the women of Moab; the name of the one was Orpah, and thename of the other Ruth: and they dwelled there about ten years. 5 And Mahlon and Chilion died also both of them; and the woman was left of her two sons and her husband... 19 So they two went until they came to Bethlehem. And it came to pass, when they were come to Bethlehem, that all the city was moved about them, and they said, Is this Naomi? 20 And she said unto them, Call me not Naomi, call me Mara: for the Almighty hath dealt very bitterly with me. 21 I went out full, and the LORD hath brought me home again empty: why then call ye me Naomi, seeing the LORD hath testified against me, and the Almighty hath afflicted me?"

The story is about an elderly woman who suffered several calamities within so short a period. Within a space of ten years, she lost her husband & two adult sons - all in a foreign land - far away from home! This must have been overwhelming for her!

Perhaps you wonder how & where this is connected with thanksgiving, it will soon be clear to you.

First, take a look at your life in the last ten years: Where were you a decade ago? Begin to recount all the blessings God had poured on you between then & now (say, 2005-2015) - you may need to get a sheet of paper. I did so too some time ago. Let me give you some Hints:

+ Where have you been or lived in the last ten years?

+ Look at events & things that had happened - in your family. That you are alive & well, that you have easy access to provisions, protection, promotions & enlargements, to education, marriage, children, etc. - Are you grateful to God?

+ What about the 'divine enablements': your career, ministry, academics: promotions, favours, etc.?+ You may want to look at your growth: physical, academic, spiritual, Books written, house (s) built, etc.

+ Have you travelled at all, or made some journeys / journeys - in the last ten years? From where to where, & by what means?

+ Take a look at the favours & divine interventions, etc, you received.

Of course, may be there were one or two unpleasant experiences you had, still you need to be grateful to God for them all. Rom 8:28, says:

"28 And we know that all things work together for good to them that love God, to them who are the called according to his purpose."

God's Time-table (Eccle 3:1-8):

"1 To every thing there is a season, and a time to every purpose under the heaven: 2 A time to be born, and a time to die; a time to plant, and a time to pluck up that which is planted; 3 A time to kill, and a time to heal; a time to break down, and a time to build up; 4 A time to weep, and a time to laugh; a time to mourn, and a time to dance; 5 A time to cast away stones, and a time to gather stones together; a time to embrace, and a time to refrain from embracing; 6 A time to get, and a time to lose; a time to keep, and a time to cast away; 7 A time to rend, and a time to sew; a time to keep silence, and a time to speak; 8 A time to love, and a time to hate; a time of war, and a time of peace."

God created the concept of time. He has power over it - control it, ignore, reverse, fast-forward, or still it.

God also has a time-Table. A Table on which He has divinely allocated events, activities, & assignments.

God's Time-table is tied to the Heavenly Calendar

The world (- it's people & events) is like a grand play or Drama with the timing of each act/scene & the role of each actor spelt out by the Divine Writer - God Himself. Eccles 3:1-8 makes it very clear that there is time for everything - a time to be born, a time to die, a time to laugh, a time for war & a time for peace. There is also a time for the rise & fall of individuals, leaders, organizations, & even Nations!

There are 'critical' times in the lives of individual human beings - a time for Salvation, deliverance, judgment, favour, fulfillment of prophecies, etc.

When the time of favour comes, some definite things will & must happen. For e.g., divine intervention takes place, you will be located (posted/positioned rightly or sought for), you will experience divine interest/remembrance - especially by a higher authority! All things will work out for your good (Rom 8:28).

Of course, when the time of fulfillment of prophecy comes, some things will & must happen: Natural laws will be suspended for your sake, protocols will be broken, ways will be made for you where there was none before, you will be connected with Divine/Destiny Helpers, your journey to destiny will be accelerated.

Prayers

- Father, thank You for Your Master plan & purpose for my life.

- Father, please help me to recognize my time & maximize it for Your glory.

- Father, arise & have mercy on me. Let this moment - day, hour, week, month, year & season be my time of favour, a time of divine intervention, location, remembrance, & divine interest.

- Father, let this hour, today, this week, month, & year be my time of fulfillment of divine prophecy.

- Father, suspend/break all natural laws & protocols & make ways for me. Connect me with my divine & destiny helpers.

- Father, accelerate my journey to success. Crush, & arrest every force working or trying to hinder Your agenda for my life (see Psalm 89:22-24).

- Father, let the time of judgment come today, this week/month & year to all enemies of my progress, peace & joy - whoever & wherever they are!

The power of Vision (John 9:1-11; Prov 29:18)

"1 And as Jesus passed by, he saw a man which was blind from his birth. 2 And his disciples asked him, saying, Master, who did sin, this man, or his parents, that he was

born blind? 3 Jesus answered, Neither hath this man sinned, nor his parents: but that the works of God should be made manifest in him. 4 I must work the works of him that sent me, while it is day: the night cometh, when no man can work. 5 As long as I am in the world, I am the light of the world. 6 When he had thus spoken, he spat on the ground, and made clay of the spittle, and he anointed the eyes of the blind man with the clay, 7 And said unto him, Go, wash in the pool of Siloam, (which is by interpretation, Sent.) He went his way therefore, and washed, and came seeing. 8 The neighbours therefore, and they which before had seen him that he was blind, said, Is not this he that sat and begged? 9 Some said, This is he: others said, He is like him: but he said, I am he. 10 Therefore said they unto him, How were thine eyes opened? 11 He answered and said, A man that is called Jesus made clay, and anointed mine eyes, and said unto me, Go to the pool of Siloam, and wash: and I went and washed, and I received sight...Where there is no vision, the people perish: but he that keepeth the law, happy is he."

Power

The power of a thing refers to the inherent ability it has to do or not to do something. It also means what it has the capability to turn whatever it comes in contact with into. Fore.g., an Airplane. It has great power to travel fast in space. It can also carry a large number of passengers as well as goods. It therefore has power to take a man from point A to point B within so short a space of time. Money too has power! Even though money has a lot of limitations, there is no doubt that money is very powerful. It can do quiet a lot! of course, money can turn men into something else. It has made some men to take on addition wives (or concubines), while it has made some ministers of true Gospel to change their message of holiness & heaven mindedness to motivational talks so they can attract & retain large crowd with itching ears!

Vision

This has been described as the ability to 'see' what ordinary eyes cannot see. It is also called a mental picture of a desired future. That future can be the next minute, tomorrow, next week, the coming month or year, or several years to come. In Gen 15: 8-16, God in a vision, spoke to the man Abraham about what would happen to his children in their fourth generation to up to four hundred years!

Vision is more that just a mere dream. It can change everything about a man - his attitude to life, money, time management, etc. Someone defined vision as "as that which you see which later take sleep from your eyes. I seem to agree with this definition because the vision the man Saul of Tarsus (who later became the great Apostle

Paul) saw on his way to Damascus (Acts 9:1-9) took all sleep away from his eyes. It also changed everything about him, & that forever! One of the things a vision of Heaven will do to a man is that he will never want to touch anything sinful or anything that has an appearance of evil.

There are various forms of vision. A vision can be physical, mental or spiritual. What can help your vision

The first & foremost thing you must do is get right with God & live a God-fearing life. In Prov 14:34, the Bible says "Righteousness exalteth a nation: but sin is a reproach to any people".

Sin & all forms of unrighteousness is an individual matter. It is destructive:

"23 For the wages of sin is death; but the gift of God is eternal life through Jesus Christ our Lord." (Rom 6:23)

It is the aggregate sin & unrighteousness of a group of people that amounts to national sins, which end up becoming a reproach to such a people &/or nations. In addition to being a reproach, sin balsa tilts or distorts a man's senses. It makes a man insensitive to right & wrong. Sin attacks & enslaves the spirit, soul & body of a person. Sin will not let you see the plan & purpose of God for your life. Sin is a destiny waster! Are you living in sin? You must get out of it if you desire to to fulfill your destiny.

Second, you must learn to read the right things. The first & best to read is the word of God - Holy Bible. From my personal experience, & the testimonies of some truly great people in history, it has become very evident that the Destiny of every man is hidden in this special Book called The Holy Bible! (Our Daddy, the G.O. of the RCCG, told us of the story surrounding his PhD thesis (in Mathematics): one night before going to bed, he decided to read his Bible. The passage that day was Exod 14 which detailed the Crossing of the Red Sea by the Israelites. According to Daddy G.O, as he was about to close his Bible & pray, the Holy Spirit asked him to take a closer look at the story.

There he began to see the event in some new light: Moses lifted up his hands; the Red Sea divided into two, & the Israelites with passed through. Then Moses lifted up hishand again & the water closed up. So, the Lord asked him to divided the complex equation he had been battling with into two, solve each separately, &'then merge the two answers together. He did so, & Hours later, he was sure God had seen him through a problem of several months.

I heard the story of a Christian Sister. She had been praying: "Lord, please show me what you want me to pursue as a career". After a few weeks the Lord made it clear to her that He (the Almighty God) had already spoken to her through the Scriptures on one the days in the week. She re breed that she had eralier read & meditated on Rom 12:14, where the Bible had said:

"So then every one of us shall give account of himself to God."

It became clear to her that God wanted her to study Accounting. She later got admitted for it & became a qualified Chattered Accountant!

By God's special grace I too can look back & recognize how God had been unfolding His redemptive purpose & plans for my life through His word. I pray that as you too become a lover of God's word, your destiny shall be revealed to you & you will also be enabled to fulfill it in Jesus Name. You need this in order to be who God made you to be & do what He created you to do!:

"18 Open thou mine eyes, that I may behold wondrous things out of thy law..9 But as it is written, Eye hath not seen, nor ear heard, neither have entered into the heart of man, the things which God hath prepared for them that love him.10 But God hath revealed them unto us by his Spirit: for the Spirit searcheth all things, yea, the deep things of God. 11 For what man knoweth the things of a man, save the spirit of man which is in him? even so the things of God knoweth no man, but theSpirit of God...God saved you by his grace when you believed. And you can't take credit for this; it is a gift from God. Salvation is not a reward for the good things we have done, so none of us can

boast about it. For we are God's masterpiece. He has created us anew in Christ Jesus, so we can do the good things he planned for us long ago." (Psalm 119:18; I Cor 2:9-11; & Ephes 2:8-10 NLT).

Still on what to read, you must get the writings of godly men. Their lives & testimonies will widen your horizon.

Third, prayer is vital to destiny fulfillment. It should be noted that Satan does not want you to ever discover your purpose in life, talk less of wanting you to fulfill it! There are a million & one things that the devil can bring your way in order to prevent you from reaching your goal. That you even succeeded in having a glimpse of your destiny is enough to make the devil mad at you. So, he will try all he can to ensure you either derail or you don't make it. Where then does prayer come in? Prayer is a summon to a higher authority for assistance. In this case the Higher Authority we are summoning is the Almighty God Himself. He has promised to hear & answer whenever & wherever we call upon Him (Psalm 119:18; Jer 33:3; Matthew 7:7-11; John 14:13-14; John 16:24; Isa 65:24). In or through prayers, you must call upon Him for leading, guidance, & for help to hinder the devil from interrupting God's agenda for your life (Lam 3:37; Pro 19:21; LUKE 10:19).

Fourth, you need the help of the Holy Spirit - in in discovering as well as in fulfilling your destiny (I Cor 2:9-

11). Fifth, you must WATCH the company you keep! Don't join the 'No future Association' group (Psalm 1:1-3; I Cor 15:33). Sixth, be diligent! God does not bless the lazy! He blesses the diligent & hard working Pro 22:29 says:"29 Seest thou a man diligent in his business? he shall stand before kings; he shall not stand before mean men."

Diligence & hard work also bring about maturity & mastery. They make us effective & efficient, they enhance our productive capacities.

Seventh, are the twin issues of obedience & faithfulness. Obedience & faithfulness in all assignments or opportunities God brings your way is very critical. God uses our obedience & faithfulness to enlarge our coasts & take us further in our journey to destiny Gen 3:1-7; I Sam 16:7-13; LUKE 16:1-3, 10-13).

May be you want to pray, that:

- God will reconnect you with Himself, & that He will cleanse you from all your sins (see Rom 3:23; Rom 6:23; Prov 28:13; I JOHN 1:5-9).

Also, ask God to take away every blockage in your eyes, ears, mind & spirit that can prevent you from discovering the purpose of God for your life.

1. Are you ready (for the Rapture)? (I Thess 4:13-18)

'Are you': This is a very personal question, & it should/must be answered personally & sincerely. When confronted with direct & personalized questions like this, many ,dodge it, some will take it as being meant for another person. Some other people will rationalize it, while some will take it casual & for granted. Only a few serious minded people will answer it candidly & sincerely (see I Cor 11:27-30). I urge you not to deceive yourself or allow anyone to deceive you through anything, or try to make you think you are o.k!

The reason to be frank with oneself is that God (& NOT) a man is the One who will do the Final markings (Rev 23:10-12). It isnot a leader, not a colleague, not a subordinate, not a friend, not a spouse, not or an enemy, & of course, not even Satan or an angel who will do the Final markings. It is God Himself!

Again, HE asks: 'Are you ready?' -

- what does it mean to be ready?:- It means to be prepared or be equipped & available at very short notice for an action. That action can be to move (e.g, stand up, walk, run, fly, fight, stop, be quiet, etc).

- Ready for what & for whom? In the scriptures we are asked to be ready for many things. For example, we are to be readily hospitable, do good, seek the Lord, confess our sins & seek forgiveness, forgive others who sin against us, & so on (see Gen 18:1-8; Gal 6:9-19; Isa 55:6-7; Prov 28:13; Matt 18: 21-22, 28-30). Here (in I Thess 4:13-18), we are being specifically asked to be ready for death, rapture, or a transfer to an eternal realm. Any of this could come or occur with little or no notice at all. Also, we are being asked here to ready for a Person - our Lord Jesus - to meet & go with Him at His soon coming (see John 14:1-3).

- What are the benefits of being ready? John 2:28-29 tells us very clearly: *"28 And now, little children, abide in him; that, when he shall appear, we may have confidence, and not be ashamed before him at his coming. 29 If ye know that he is righteous, ye know that every one that doeth righteousness is born of him."* Generally speaking, there is a degree of confidence that accompanies readiness in whatever a man is involved in. The Bible says here that whey you are continually right with God & by His grace daily prepared for His appearing, you will be confident & unashamed when He finally appears! May this be our portion in Jesus Name. In addition, you will also receive your rewards (- a 'well done', & crowns). In other words, he Or she who is ready will laugh last!

- What are the dangers of not being ready? They are many. The greatest & most terrible is that of eternal

The Almighty Formulae

separation from God, & loved ones; burning in Hell for ever & eternal regret (MAY GOD HAVE MERCY)!

- How do I get ready? (a) know what to be ready in or about; (b) know the pass mark or cut off point (c) know the deadline & target or submission date.

- Why many are not ready or will not be ready? There could be several reasons. For example, ignorance, - ignorance of what to be ready about & how to be ready, as well as the benefits of being ready, & the dangers of not being ready). On many occasions, Apostle Paul particularly warned Brethren against Ignorance (see I Cor 12:1; I Thess 4:1; I Cor 14:38; Acts 17: 30, etc). A lot of questions can agitate one's mind when it comes to the subject of ignorance. For example, what is ignorance?, why is it dangerous?, what are the dangers of ignorance?, what are we not to be ignorant of/or about? Many things, but especially (1) God's Calendar & timing. God's timing & calendar differ greatly from our earthly timing & calendar: *"8 But, beloved, be not ignorant of this one thing, that one day is with the Lord as a thousand years, and a thousand years as one day. 9 The Lord is not slack concerning his promise, as some men count slackness; but is longsuffering to us-ward, not willing that any should perish, but that all should come to repentance."* (II Peter 3:8-9). The Bible seem to be saying here that 1 day with God is 1,000 Years, &

1,000 years is as 1 day! This means for example, that 2,015 years (since CHRIST went) is just 2Hrs+ a few seconds! It also means that a man who is 63 years of age, is just 1Hr+ 30.72mins! The implications of this are many both physically & especially, spiritually. A man who is 63 years old is like a brand new baby before God. Such a baby doesn't know his right from my left. He must learn to depend on God for all he needs (Psalm 127:1; John 15:5). If he is humble, meek & holy, God can carry him in His mighty Arms. In view of this (knowledge), Such a man must be wise to live right 24/7! - never on holiday or recess for a second/minute. He must also learn to take serious, the words of Rom 12:1-2:*"1 I beseech you therefore, brethren, by the mercies of God, that ye present your bodies a living sacrifice, holy, acceptable unto God, which is your reasonable service. 2. And be not conformed to this world: but be ye transformed by the renewing of your mind, that ye may prove what is that good, and acceptable, and perfect, will of God."*

- Know ye not (that you are the temple of the Holy Spirit)? Taken along with the earlier one (on 'Are You a Ready'), 'know ye not' is a personal matter - it is focused on 'you' & not on other people. Also, it is not on Ministry work. BUT on you. Hence, the need to pay attention & take it serious!: **"24 *Know ye not that they which run in a race run all, but one receiveth the prize? So run, that ye*** *may obtain. 25 And every man that striveth for the mastery is temperate in all things. Now they do it to obtain a corruptible crown; but we an incorruptible. 26 I therefore so run, not as uncertainly; so fight I, not as one that beateth the air: 27 But I keep under my body, and bring it into subjection: lest that by any means, when I have preached to others, I myself should be a castaway....28 And now, little children, abide in him; that, when he shall appear, we may have confidence, and not be ashamed before him at his coming. 29 If ye know that he is righteous, ye know that every one that doeth righteousness is born of him."* (I Cor 9:24-27; I John 2:28-29).

'You are' - This is not a question. It is unlike 'Are You...'? Rather, it is an affirmation. It is a call to an understanding of self - a call to realize & maximize who God made you to be. It is critical to know who God says you are & be who He says you are! Don't live in ignorance or abuse yourself thereby wasting God's grace & investment on you!

'You are': God made you many things. First, He made you in His image & likeness. You are a masterpiece! (Gen 1:26-28; Ephes 2:8-10 NLT). Also, He made you a 'tripartite' being - spirit, soul & body. Furthermore, you are His beloved - the Apple of His eyes. Above all (as focused here), your body is God's Sanctuary, His Temple - where His Holy Spirit dwells! Let's look at this more closely - the fact that you are the Sanctuary & Temple of God:

- What does one expect to find in a temple - God's temple (& not a shrine)?: Among others, one expects to find God's presence & glory, His holiness; worship (praise, thanksgiving, & gifts brought to sacrifice to God, etc). One also expects to find prayers (in all forms) as well as testimonies. Of course, one will look round to see if there is an Altar. Finally, His power, & His Angels, etc.

- What are the things one does not expect to find in a temple - God's temple? - Things such as uncleanness, idolatry, sin, hypocrisy, lying, fornication, adultery, any form of abomination, etc are to be far away from a place or person that is described as God's Temple. Ephes 5:1-7 says: *"1 Be ye therefore followers of God, as dear children; 2 And walk in love, as Christ also hath loved us, and hath given himself for us an offering and a sacrifice to God for a sweetsmelling savour. 3 But fornication, and all uncleanness, or covetousness, let it not be once named among you, as becometh saints; 4 Neither filthiness, nor foolish talking, nor jesting, which are not convenient: but rather giving of thanks. 5 For this ye know, that no whoremonger, nor unclean person, nor covetous man, who is an idolater, hath any inheritance in the kingdom of Christ and of God. Live in the Light. 6 Let no man deceive you with vain words: for because of these things cometh the wrath of God upon the children of disobedience. 7 Be not ye therefore partakers with them. 8 For ye were sometimes darkness, but now are ye light in the Lord: walk as children of light."* (See Acts 5:1-11).

- The questions then arise: Are what should be found in God's Temple found in me? Also, are what should not be found in God's temple found in me? - These call for a thorough & personal check up (see I John 2:28-29).

- What are we to do? This will largely upon your personal state. Generally speaking, the First step may be that of rebuilding the Altar, this is preparatory to bringing back the King (see II Kings 18:25-38; II Sam 6:1-14). Knowledge is power! It has a lot of benefits - particularly the knowledge of who you are. It will help you to know your strengths & weaknesses, your limitations & boundaries. This will assist you to administer yourself - you will not over or underrate yourself, & you will not exceed your own elastic limit.

Finally, you will not compare yourself with others, an act the Bible describe as foolish (see...).

- Do you know who you are? You are the Temple of the Holy Spirit - one in whom He wants to dwell, through whom He wants to manifest Himself,(His fruit & gifts), through whom He wants to glorify JESUS,

- How then are you to treat your body? You are to treat it with dignity & honour. Stop abusing & misusing it (both as a whole &/or its parts). Keep it clean (not polluting/ contaminating) it, or pairing it up with harlots & evil doers. You are also to guard each part of your body - you are to take concrete actions to forbid further invasion &/or advancement of the adversary in

Afterwords

The Almighty God has not changed. He does not change. He will not change - both in nature, character & power. He is eve r willing, wanting & waiting to help His own children & people. How has been your relationship with Him. Do you yet know Him? Are you His true child (Nahum 1:7; I John 3:7-10; John 14:21-23)? Perhaps you once knew Him, but you discarded Him for other gods (both physical & spiritual) that are more convenient & which meet or suits you - the gods you can order around at will! The truth you need to face is that you need the true God. He is your hope. Without Him life itself has no meaning, because He is the real life.

Having gone through this book thus far, I believe you would have discovered that He is real, alive & well. I implore you to take your relationship with this ALMIGHTY God very serious. This could only be done through studying His word

- the Holy Bible, & by your life of obedience. As you obey Him, your life will become radiant (Psalm

119:130) & obstacles in your way will melt. Isa 60:1-3 says:

"1 Arise, shine; for thy light is come, and the glory of the LORD is risen upon thee. 2 For, behold, the darkness shall cover the earth, and gross darkness the people: but the LORD shall arise upon thee, and his glory shall be seen upon thee. 3 And the Gentiles shall come to thy light, and kings to the brightness of thy rising."

So, ARISE!

THE END

Acknowledgments

I give all the glory to God for making possible, the writing of yet another book. He is my **Inspirer.** I thank all God's true children whom He gave me the benefit of knowing & learning from over the years.

In particular, I specially thank my spiritual parents - Pastors Folu & Enoch Adeboye (Wife & General Overseer, The Redeemed Christian Church of God (TRCCG). Much of the materials that appear in this book (especially towards the end of this book under **"Matters Arising"**, have been inspired/provoked as the Lord took me through some editions of the Daily Devotional **"OPEN HEAVENS"** written by our Daddy). Daddy & Mummy, may both of you finish well & finish strong. May you end your earthly race without any scars.

I thank Brethren at all levels in RCCG (Australia/Pacific) Region including Lawrence Eguae of Sydney, Tunde & Kemi Fadahunsi of Perth, WA; Silaulelei & Mafumaiala Asaua of Samoa, etc. Also, I greatly thank Wale & Bukola Omolokun of Melbourne.

Finally, Great thanks to God for my wife, Jane Adesola, as well as God's gifts to us - Tolulope & Temitope Haastrup. May you all continue to experience the greatness of God in your lives as you too obey Him. To God be all the glory.

'Wole Haastrup,
11/12/15.

www.ingramcontent.com/pod-product-compliance
Lightning Source LLC
Chambersburg PA
CBHW070428010526
44118CB00014B/1949